en: art of nexus | e

Padiglione Giappone
Biennale Architettura 2016

-001

en: art of nexus

—

First published in Japan
on April 25, 2016

—

Second published
on March 1, 2018

—

Edited by
Yoshiyuki Yamana,
Seiichi Hishikawa,
Masaki Uchino,
and Masatake Shinohara

—

Publisher:
Toru Kato

—

TOTO Publishing (TOTO LTD.)
TOTO Nogizaka Bldg. 2F
1-24-3 Minami-Aoyama
Minato-ku, Tokyo
107-0062, Japan
[Sales]
Telephone: +81-3-3402-7138
Facsimile: +81-3-3402-7187
[Editorial]
Telephone: +81-3-3497-1010
URL: https://jp.toto.com/publishing

—

Book Designer:
Yuzo Kariya+Nao Kakuta / neucitora

—

Printer:
Tosho Printing Co., LTD.

Except as permitted under copyright law,
this book may not be reproduced,
in whole or in part, in any form or by any means,
including photocopying, scanning,
digitizing, or otherwise, without prior permission.
Scanning or digitizing this book through
a third party, even for personal or home use,
is also strictly prohibited.
The list price is indicated on the cover.

—

ISBN978-4-88706-358-7

en: art of nexus
—

en［縁］：アート・オブ・ネクサス
—

［編］

山名善之

菱川勢一

内野正樹

篠原雅武
—

Edited by

Yoshiyuki Yamana,

Seiichi Hishikawa,

Masaki Uchino,

and Masatake Shinohara

en: art of nexus

-003

TOTO出版

en［縁］:アート・オブ・ネクサス

山名善之

若年層を中心に失業が慢性化し、格差や貧困の度合いが日々昂進している今日の日本において、戦後の「高度経済成長」はもはや遠い過去の歴史的事象のようなものとなっている。近代日本の「経済成長」とともにつくり出された建築作品のいくつかは世界に誇れるものであったが、日本における近代建築の輝かしい成果は、前回のヴェネチア・ビエンナーレの日本館において「現代建築の倉」に収蔵され、「高度経済成長」をピークに生み出された建築作品の数々はすでに歴史家たちの対象となっている。

情報環境を劇的に変化させたインターネットの普及など、われわれの時代の指標となる事象はさまざまにあるが、競争原理をその核にすえた新自由主義は、戦争やテロ、放射性物質による環境汚染などと異なり目の前の脅威としては捉えにくいものの、いまや社会の隅々にまで浸透してその屋台骨を深く蝕んでいる。

そしてさらに3.11以降の喪失感が加わった中で日本の社会はいま、大きな転換期を迎えている。このような時代に、われわれの建築はどのようにつくられているのか。そしてまた、どこへ向かおうとしているのか。われわれがいま注目するのは、その多くが、建築のメディアを華やかに飾るようにも、また、これまでの建築の枠組みを大きく変えるようにも、少なくとも表面上においては見えない建築群である。その理由のひとつは、人と人、モノとモノ、そして人とモノの結びつき──すなわち、本展のテーマである「縁」をつくること、「縁」を変えることに重点を置いているから、と考えられる。

本展では、なんらかの旗印のもと、モダン・ムーヴメントに見られたような運動体を形成することなく、直面した状況課題に対して、それぞれ個々に戦われている戦いの多様な様相を見てみようと思う。われわれが置かれた困難な状況を超えて生き延びるためのこの最前線での戦いは、まだ胎動を始めたばかりのものが多いかもしれないが、さまざまな結びつき(nexus)に着目しながら生み出された本展の作品群は、社会変革のベースをつくっていく、そんな潜在可能性をもっている。

en: *art of nexus*

Yoshiyuki Yamana

In contemporary Japan, where unemployment, particularly among the young, has become chronic, and inequality and poverty grow worse every day, the high-growth economy of the postwar era is now a historical event that belongs to the distant past. There are several world-renowned works of architecture that emerged in tandem with economic growth in modern Japan. But the brilliant achievements of Japanese modern architecture have already been summed in *In the Real World*, an exhibition held in the Japan Pavilion at the last Venice Biennale, and many architectural works that emerged at the height of the growth period are now subjects for historians.

Various phenomena act as an index of our times, such as the popularization of the Internet and other developments that have dramatically altered the information environment. But neoliberalism, rooted in the principle of competition, has deeply eroded every corner of the social framework, despite the fact that it does not appear to be an immediate threat like war, terrorism or environmental pollution caused by radioactive materials.

With the additional sense of loss that arose in the aftermath of the Great East Japan Earthquake, which occurred on March 11, 2011, Japanese society is currently on the verge of a huge turning point. How is our architecture changing to fit this new era? Where exactly is our architecture headed? Whether it concerns the beautiful ornamentation of the medium or the drastic modification of an existing framework, many of the things we focus on here are not visible on a superficial level in the works. This is in part due to our emphasis on the links between people, things, and people and things – in other words, the primary theme of this exhibition is the importance of creating and changing *en*.

This exhibition does not attempt to formulate a vehicle, such as those seen in Modernism, which set out to convey some kind of big story or slogan. Instead, it examines a variety of aspects related to individual struggles in the fight against conditions and issues that we are currently confronting. Though this fight, being waged on the front lines to ensure that we can survive these difficult conditions, may be in its infancy, the group of works presented in this exhibition, which focuses on a variety of *en*, has the latent potential to serve as a basis for social change.

目次

en［縁］：アート・オブ・ネクサス｜山名善之 —————————————— 004

縁の空間論｜篠原雅武 —————————————————————— 008

人の縁 ———————————————————————————— 020

不動前ハウス｜常山未央／mnm ——————————————————— 024

ヨコハマアパートメント｜西田司＋中川エリカ ——————————————— 032

LT城西｜成瀬・猪熊建築設計事務所 ——————————————————— 040

食堂付きアパート｜仲建築設計スタジオ —————————————————— 048

モノの縁 ——————————————————————————— 056

高岡のゲストハウス｜能作アーキテクツ —————————————————— 060

駒沢公園の家｜今村水紀＋篠原勲／miCo. ————————————————— 068

15Aの家｜レビ設計室 ————————————————————————— 076

躯体の窓｜増田信吾＋大坪克亘 ————————————————————— 084

渥美の床 他｜403 architecture［dajiba］ —————————————————— 092

調布の家｜青木弘司建築設計事務所 ——————————————————— 102

地域の縁 ——————————————————————————— 110

神山町プロジェクト｜BUS ——————————————————————— 114

馬木キャンプ｜美井戸神社｜ドットアーキテクツ —————————————— 126

展示デザイン｜teco ————————————————————————— 136

新自由主義へのミクロな抵抗｜佐藤嘉幸 ——————————————— 146

プロフィール —————————————————————————————— 152

クレジット ——————————————————————————————— 159

Contents

en: *art of nexus* | **Yoshiyuki Yamana** — 005

The *En* Spatial Theory | **Masatake Shinohara** — 009

The *En* of People — 020

House for Seven People | **Mio Tsuneyama /mnm** — 024

Yokohama Apartments | **Osamu Nishida ＋ Erika Nakagawa** — 032

LT Josai | **Naruse Inokuma Architects** — 040

Apartments with a Small Restaurant | **Naka Architects' Studio** — 048

The *En* of Things — 056

Guest House in Takaoka | **Nousaku Architects** — 060

House at Komazawa Park | **Mizuki Imamura＋Isao Shinohara/miCo.** — 068

15A House | **Levi Architecture** — 076

Boundary Window | **Shingo Masuda＋Katsuhisa Otsubo Architects** — 084

The Floor of Atsumi, etc. | **403 architecture [dajiba]** — 092

House in Chofu | **Koji Aoki Architects** — 102

The *En* of Locality — 110

Projects in Kamiyama | **BUS** — 114

Umaki Camp | Beat Shrine | **dot architects** — 126

Venue Design | **teco** — 136

A Micro-resistance to Neoliberalism | Yoshiyuki Sato — 147

Profile — 152

Credits — 159

縁の空間論

篠原雅武

1

- 縁は、日常的に使用される日本語である。この言葉は、仏教に由来するが、西洋の影響下で生活習慣がつくり変えられていく過程を経た現代においても、普通に使われている。

- 縁は、人間生活の条件にかかわる不可思議なことを意味する言葉である。そこにはふたつの意味がある。

a 原因を助けて結果を生じさせる作用。間接的原因。思いもよらない偶然の関係。

b ゆかり。つづきあい。関係。

a 縁は、世の中は偶然の出会いに満ちているという信念に、対応する言葉である。そして、偶然の出会いを大切にし、一緒に生きていこうという心持ちに対応する言葉である。旅先でたまたま出会った人との縁を大切にする心持ちや、迎え入れてもらった集団の中でいただいた縁に感謝し一緒に暮らそうという気持ちなど、縁を大切にするという気持ちが、古来より日本人の深層意識に根差している。人との出会いや出来事は、理性的な計画図や定めに従うものではなく、「おのずから次々に生成していく」ようにしてたまたま起きているという思いがある。人が生きるとは、この生成の中に身をさらし、人や出来事との出会いの度ごとに判断し、良いと思われる方向へと軌道修正することである。明日はどうなるか分からなくても、日々の偶然と付き合いつつさらなる展開を起こすことでしか世の中は動かないと、私たちは信じようとする。

- 縁は、次々と起こる出会いや出来事を、それらが偶然のことのように思われたとしても、可能な限りで受け入れていこうとする心意気に対応する言葉である。この態度は、何であろうと潜在的には相互に連関しているという直観に根差している。とはいえ、出会いや出来事は、あくまでも潜在的に連関しているだけである。この連関が現実の建造環境となって成立するためには、出会いや出来事を、関わらせ、繋ぎ、重ね合わせ、共存させていこうとする実践が欠かせない。この実践は、関係と共存の場を錯綜体としてつく

The *En* Spatial Theory

Masatake Shinohara

1

— The character 縁, *en*, is in common use in Japanese. While its origins lie in Buddhism and today's Japanese lifestyles have changed under Western influences, it remains an everyday part of Japanese discourse and behavior.

— *En* means something mysterious that affects the conditions of human life. It has two major interpretations.

a) An action that aids a cause in generating an effect. An indirect cause. An utterly unexpected, curious coincidence.

b) Connection, affinity, relationship, edges.

a) In the first sense, *en* is a term associated with the belief that the world is filled with fortuitous encounters. It corresponds to the feeling that we will treasure those fortuitous encounters and live on, involved with each other. The feelings of valuing a connection formed with a person unexpectedly encountered on a journey, of being grateful for the *en* of jointing a group in which one has been included, of treasuring *en* are deeply rooted in the Japanese consciousness, with origins in the distant past. The idea is that encounters with others do not follow a rational plan or rule but just happen, "Coming about by themselves, one after another." Human beings discover themselves within that process, judge each encounter with each other, each event, and adjust their paths to move in a direction perceived as good. Not knowing what tomorrow will bring, we try to believe that we can change the world only through further developments caused by our associations with the random chances each day brings.

— *En* is a word that corresponds to the kindness to accept, as much as possible, encounters and events as they occur, even if they seem to be random or accidental. This attitude is rooted in the intuition that all events and things are interconnected at the ontological level. But encounters and events are only potentially related. For such interconnections to come into existence as actual built environments, the practices of connecting, linking, stacking, encouraging encounters and events are indispensable. Those practices are concerned with the roots of architecture, the creation and maintenance of a nexus of relationship and coexistence as complex units.

b) In its second sense, *en* means "edge" or "margin." Here *en* are boundaries that surround a certain locus of

り出し維持するという、建築の根幹にかかわる。

b 縁は、「へり」や「ふち」を意味する言葉でもある。一定の生活の場の周囲を取りまく
境界だが、場を閉ざすのではない。生活の場を、外の世界へと開き、内と外とが相
互に作用し接触していくことを促す曖昧な境目である。

— 西欧的な認識では、境界は、部屋の壁や城壁のように、区別し切断するものとして捉
えられる。これに対して日本語の「縁」が意味する「へり」や「ふち」は、異なる領域を、
区別はしても連関させて相互浸透させるものとして考えられている。この相互浸透的な
場が、人のふるまいを触発し、人を出会わせ、関係形成を促していく。「へり」や「ふち」
に対応するのは、縁側、窓、廊下、階段、踊り場、道といった空間である。

— 「へり」や「ふち」が、人や事物を偶然に出会わせ、関係性と出会いの場を、思いもよ
らない方向や規模へと広げていくということに素直に従うという心づもりは、現代のイン
ターネットの発展とともに実感される相互連関や偶然の出会いの増殖と符合している。
ただし縁は、あくまでも「へり」や「ふち」として、建築的に表現される。

2

— 縁が建築をつくり、建築が縁をつくる。ゆえに、本展示の建築群は、「縁の建築」と名
付けることができる。

— 「縁の建築」群が建てられていくことの過程は、すでにある建物、すでにある街並み、そ
こで生きていた人びと、建築を取りまく環境、地域との出会いから始まる。

— 建築家たちは、そこにあるもの、生きている人びと、場所、状況、雰囲気と向き合う。具
体物としての建物と場所を観察するが、それだけでなく、その場所に独自の個性を与
えている質感および時間を感じ取ろうとする。そして、そこに住み、生活している人たち
の話を聴き、さらにこれから住むことになる人たちの生活を想像していく。図面を引き、
既存の建物や場所に対して建築を通じた働きかけを始めると、モノとモノとの相互作
用が発生する。その過程で、建築家は、モノの履歴や住人の記憶を発見し、新しい
価値を見出していく。生きられてきた建物の確かな質感、
事物がたたえる時の持続に気づかされていく。古くからある
モノの分解と転用、再構成、古いモノと新しいモノの結合、

living, but they do not close that locus off. These ambiguous boundary lines open places to the outside world and encourage contacts in which inside and outside act on each other.

— In Western thinking, boundaries are regarded as distinguishing and isolating places, like the walls of a room or castle walls. In contrast, the meaning of "edge" or "margin" in the Japanese word *en* is regarded as facilitating interpenetration between differing terrains, while also distinguishing between them. As a permeable boundary, *en* triggers human behavior and encourages encounters between people and the formation of relationships. That sense of *en* is seen in the spaces we call verandas, windows, hallways, stairways, landings, and roads.

— Edges and margins make possible random encounters between people and things and expand the site of relationships and encounters in unexpected directions and on unexpected scales. The expectation that one will simply follow where those developments lead coincides with the multiplication of reciprocal relations and accidental encounters we experience today with the development of the internet. *En*, however, is expressed architecturally as edges and margins, come what may.

2

— *En* defines architecture; architecture builds *en*. Thus, we can give the name "*En* architecture" to the group of architectural works in this exhibition.

— The process by which this "*En* architecture" group came about begins with encounters: encounters with existing buildings, existing townscapes, the people who live there, and the locality, the environmental context surrounding architecture.

— Architects confront what is there: people, places, circumstances, atmosphere. They observe a building and a place as tangible things, but that is not all; they attempt to sense the texture and the flow of time that give that place its specific character. Then architects listen to the people who reside there, who make their lives there, and imagine the lifestyles of the people who will live there in the future. In drawing plans, beginning to work on existing buildings and places through architectural practice, interactive effects between objects take place. In that process, the architect discovers the histories of objects and residents' memories and finds new values. The architect is made aware of the true texture, the sensual qualities of buildings that have been lived in, the duration of time filled with events. He or she rethinks the deconstruction, repurposing, and reconfiguration of things that have

新しい技術と古い技術の結合、建物と都市の関係性の見直し、地域との関係の再構成などの可能性に気づいていく。建築家は、人、モノ、地域の連関の過程の中へと引きずり込まれる。作家の過剰な自意識が消え、人、モノ、地域の連関、関係性を丁寧に構成していく行為者としての建築家となってふるまい始める。

— 建築ができていく過程で生活が営まれるようになると、今度は建築が縁をつくる。縁側や路地といった空間は、複数の異なる生活領域の隙間に形成されるが、この隙間が交流の場になる。また、「駒沢公園の家」の場合、ひとつの家の中には複数の部屋があるのだが、部屋は完全に閉ざされることなく半ば開かれた状態にある。この半ば開かれた状態が、家の中には他にも人がいるという気配を生じさせ、そのことで、各人が一緒に生活しているという感触の共有が可能になる。あるいは、小豆島という地域の隙間にたたずむ「馬木キャンプ」は、共に食べ、会話し、仕事をするというだけでなく、ひとりでぼんやりしていることをも許容する、緩やかな公共空間である。

— 人が出会い、共存するということは、縁により可能となる。つまり、偶然的な状況と関係に依存して起こる。縁の建築は、出会いや生活が偶然的に起こり得る状況をつくり出し確かなものにしていく。

3

— 「縁の建築」が現れてきたことの背景には、近代的な建築の支えとなった秩序への信頼の喪失がある。西洋近代との出会い以降、時空を律する等質的で透明な秩序が、建築および都市の空間構造を支えているという信念が、日本では長らく支配的であった。そして戦後日本では、高度経済成長の達成への自信から、無限の経済成長が続くと長らく信じられてきた。近代的な秩序への信頼は、経済成長への自信に裏打ちされていた。

— だが、1970年頃に世界経済が変動し、高度経済成長が終焉を迎えるのに伴い、近代的な秩序への信頼が揺らぎ始める。前衛的な近代建築運動（メタボリズム）の勢いが衰え始める。すると、建築家たちの中に、建築と実生活との関係へと関心を向ける人が出てくる。建築のあり方を、「身体性」「空間の奥行き」「モノの具体性」などとのかかわりの中で問い直そうとする人が出てくる。

existed there from the past, the combination of new and old things, the combination of new and old technologies, the relationships between architecture and the city, and takes note of the potential for reconfiguring relationships with the locality. The architect is pulled into the process of relationships with people, things and localities. The excessive self-consciousness of the auteur vanishes; the architect begins to behave as a doer thoughtfully configuring a nexus, the connections that link people, things, and locality.

— When, in the process of a building's being built, lives are lived there, then the building will go on to build *en*, connections, sharing. The spaces we call verandas and alleys are formed in the interstices between multiple different lifestyle domains. Those interstices become places for interaction. In the case of the "House at Komazawa Park," there are multiple rooms inside one house, and the rooms are not entirely shut off but halfway open. That halfway open state reminds residents that others are in the house and makes it possible to share the feeling that all of those people are living together. "Umaki Camp," which stands in an opening on a place known as Shodo Island, is a gentle public space where people can eat, talk, and work together but also where a person can relax alone.

— *En* makes it possible for people to encounter each other and live together, through connections and sharing. Its occurrence depends on improbable states and relationships. *En* architecture will reinforce that tendency, creating the circumstances in which encounters and lifestyles occur by chance.

3

— Behind the emergence of *en* architecture is a loss of trust in the order that underpinned modern architecture. Beginning with Japan's encounter with Western modernity, its transparent, uniform order governed time and space. Modernist principles long dominated architecture and the construction of urban spaces Japan. After World War II, Japan's confidence in achieving rapid economic growth led to the long-held belief that economic growth would continue without limit. Trust in the modern order was backed by confidence in economic growth.

— In the 1970s, however, the global economy changed, and Japan's period of rapid economic growth came to an end. With that change, trust in the modern order began to weaken. The avant-garde modern architecture movement (Metabolism) began to lose momentum. Some architects began directing their concern to the relationship between architecture and

— そして、近代的な建築秩序への信頼をさらに動揺させたのが、1995年の阪神淡路大震災であった。この時人びとは、「自然災害の影響を受けやすいところで生活している」ことを否応なしに知ることになる。建築家たちも、崩壊可能性を、自らの仕事の条件として受け入れていく。崩壊は、イメージのレベルではなく、「モノ」のレベルで起こる。崩壊の後の瓦礫は、私たちの生きている世界が、無数の「モノ」の連関で成り立っていることを露わにする。「モノ」の連関は、たまたま一定の状態で結合され形を成しているだけのことで、震災や戦災があれば崩壊し、連関を欠いた無数の「モノ」へと分解される。この崩壊、破壊に際しては、近代的な建築秩序は無力である。

— そして、リーマン・ショックと東日本大震災という巨大な出来事の後、近代的な建築の秩序が、またしても問い直されることになる。建築家たちは、何を建築したらよいのか、建築とは何かという問いに、直面する。

— なおも建築をするためには、既成の秩序とは違う方法を考え、さらにこの方法を、現実生活にとって意味のあるものとして定着させていかねばならない。建築家たちは、ふたつの課題に直面する。ひとつが、いかなる建築の枠組をつくるか、であり、もうひとつが、建築と現実生活との関係をどのようなものとして考えるのか、である。

— 「縁の建築家」たちは、建築の論理を、現実生活との関係の中で模索している。彼らは、人が実際に生活しているところで起きていることの水準で、建築を問い直している。そこでの重要問題は、人間が確かに生きていることを可能にしてくれる空間をつくり出すことはできるのか、というものである。人間の生活において起きているさまざまなことが生き生きとしていて、出来事がさらなる出来事を引き起こすきっかけになり、また、人と人との出会いが相互を触発し思いもよらない展開に繋がっていくような空間をつくり出すことは可能か、というものである。

— そして、「縁の建築」群が提示するのは、縁はおのずと生じるものではない、ということである。縁を生じさせ、促していくのは、人が生きていて、何かをしている過程である。もちろん、人が生きることには、理不尽、不如意、過ちがつきものである。出会いもあればすれ違いもあり、摩擦もある。ただ幸せな出会いや出来事だけでなく、悪い出来事も、縁の中には含まれる。人が生きる過程を確かなものとして支えていくためには、人が生きていて何かをしている具体的な場をつくり、支えるための建築実践が不可欠
である。そして、人のふるまいの場をつくり出すために、建築家
たちは「モノ」と向き合い、地域と向き合うことになる。

real life. Some questioned the nature of architecture in terms of its relationship with physicality, dimensions, the concreteness of things, and other concepts.

— The Great Hanshin Earthquake of 1995 further shook faith in the modern architectural order. People learned, undeniably, that "We live in a place highly vulnerable to natural disaster." Architects began to accept the possibility of collapse in the conditions for their work. Collapse is not something at the concept level; it occurs at the "real thing" level. The rubble left after collapse openly reveals that the world we live in is formed on the basis of the formation and composition of countless things. Interconnections between things give rise to forms that emerge through combinations under certain conditions and will collapse when an earthquake or a war occurs, reducing them to countless isolated things. In the face of that collapse, that destruction, the modern architectural order is powerless.

— After two more huge disasters, the global financial crisis and the Tohoku Earthquake and Tsunami, the modern architectural order was questioned yet again. Architects confronted the question of what they should build and what architecture is.

— To do architecture, it is necessary to think in ways that go beyond the established order and to establish those new ways as having meaning in real life. Architects face two issues. One is what sort of framework to build for architecture. The other is how to think about the relationship between architecture and real life.

— *En* architects are searching for architectural logic in its relationship with real life. They are questioning architecture at the level of what occurs in the places where people actually live. There the critical question is, is it possible to build spaces in which people can surely live. Is it possible to build spaces such that events in human lives scintillate, glow with life, and become the stimuli for new events, so that encounters between people trigger each other and are connected to unanticipated developments?

— What works of *En* architecture propose is that *en* does not happen by itself. The process by which humans live and do things stimulates and gives rise to *en*. Of course, things that are unreasonable, contrary to one's wishes, and erroneous are also part of human life. Encounters happen; so do occasions when people cross paths without meeting. Friction occurs. But *en* includes not only happy encounters and events but bad ones, too. Architectural practice that builds and supports physical sites where people can live and do things is an essential support for the processes of human life. And to build places where people can act and interact, architects confront the realities of "things" and localities.

016-

en: art of nexus

Padiglione Giappone Biennale Architettura 2016

-017

en: art of nexus

Padiglione Giappone Biennale Architettura 2016

-019

The En of

House for Seven People Mio Tsuneyama / mnm
Yokohama Apartments Osamu Nishida + Erika Nakagawa
LT Josai Naruse Inokuma Architects
Apartments with a Small Restaurant Naka Architects' Studio
Guest House in Takaoka Nousaku Architects
House at Komazawa Park Mizuki Imamura + Isao Shinohara / miCo.
15A House Levi Architecture
Boundary Window Shingo Masuda + Katsuhisa Otsubo Architects
The Floor of Atsumi, etc. 403 architecture [dajiba]
House in Chofu Koji Aoki Architects
Projects in Kamiyama BUS
Umaki Camp Beat Shrine dot architects

人の縁

020–

People

戦後日本で建設された都市住宅は、戸建住宅と集合住宅に大別できるが、そのほとんどが核家族に対応する。そこで重視されたのは、核家族が個々別々に自足した住宅空間の中で豊かで平和に生活するということであった。人びとは、住宅空間内に自足しつつ、他人と深くかかわることなく、軋轢や摩擦を経験せずに生きることができた。この傾向は、1980年代以降のワンルームマンション（単身者がひとりで生活するための空間）の増加へと発展する。個のための空間は、地域共同体や血縁のしがらみからの自由を実現する反面、引きこもりや密室の暴力、公共的な生活の形骸化、緩やかな交流機会の欠落という問題の要因ともなり得る。

2000年代後半辺りから、開かれた空間をつくり出そうとする機運が高まってきたのは、個へと分断された空間に特有の問題への応答として、捉えることができるだろう。つまり、住宅の中に、人の集まることのできる空間をつくり出すことで、一緒に食事をしたり、読書会をしたり、映画の上映会をするといったさまざまな「家開き」の実践が、日本の各地で始まりつつある。それは、家族や個人で自足せず、地域の人、友人などと緩やかにかかわり、共存していくことに価値を見出す人たちが出てきたことの証と言える。

この状況に関心をもつ建築家たちは、複数の人たちが生活する建築の中に、人が出会うことのできる空間を入れ込んでいく。路地や縁側、食堂、広場など、従来は外側にあるとみなされてきた空間を中へと入れ込む。これらの隙間の空間が、そこで生きている人たちおのおのの生活の個性を尊重しつつ、それを過度な摩擦や軋轢にまで発展しない程度に緩和しながら、人びとのあいだに思いもよらない出会いを発生させる触媒になる。

また、人の出会いの空間の創出は、「モノ」の連関の試みとも連動している。「食堂付きアパート」には、1階部分に共同のキッチンがあり、また1階から3階を貫く立体路地には、洗濯機やベンチといった「モノ」が設置されている。住人や地域の人たちは、これらの「モノ」を使う中で、人と出会っていく。建築家は、人の出会いの支えとなる生活習慣、生活環境が、「モノ」の連関に左右されるようになっていることにも意識的である。その点では、人の縁の空間は、「モノ」の出合いの空間、「モノ」との出合いの空間として捉えることもできるだろう。

[MS]

Urban residences built in postwar Japan can be broadly divided into single-family dwellings and housing complexes. Almost units all, however, are designed for the nuclear family. The priority was to provide residential spaces in which nuclear families could live self-sufficiently and in peace and prosperity. People were able to live autonomously in their residential spaces without deep relationships with others and without experiencing discord or friction. That trend developed, from the 1980s on, into an increase in studio apartments designed for single people living on their own. Spaces for the individual are the reverse of achieving freedom through bonds based on local communities or blood ties; they are factors behind problems such as acute social withdrawal, domestic violence, the hollowing out of public life, and the lack of opportunities for relaxed interaction with others.

Since the first years of the twenty-first century, a growing movement to build open spaces has been perceived as an answer to the problems specific to splitting spaces into individual units. Creating spaces where people can gather within residences, spaces where they can enjoy family-like activities--eating together, organizing reading circles, showing movies--is a movement that has begun throughout Japan. Its spread demonstrates the existence of people who, rather than being self sufficient as individuals or families, discover value in co-existence, in gentle relationships with neighbors and friends.

Architects interested in this situation are incorporating spaces where people can encounter each other in buildings in which numerous people live. Alleys, verandas, dining rooms, plazas: spaces conventionally regarded as being on the outside are brought inside the building. These gap spaces are catalysts for the occurrence of unexpected encounters, in a context that reduces the likelihood of excessive friction and discord, while respecting the specific character of the lifestyles of each of the residents.

The creation of spaces for human encounters is also linked to experiments with connections with "things." "Apartments with a Small Restaurant" may have a shared kitchen on the first floor, and "things," such as a washing machine or benches, placed on the three-dimensional alley running from the first through the third floor. When residents and neighbors are using those things, they encounter other people. The architects are aware that the customs and environment that sustain encounters with others are influenced by relationships with things. In that respect, the space of the *en* of people can be grasped as a space for encounters between and with things. [MS]

建築の「ふち」を調整することで、
楽しく緩い共同生活を可能に

Adjusting Architectural "Edges" to Realize
a Loose-knit and Enjoyable Communal Lifestyle

常山未央/mnm

Mio Tsuneyama/mnm

不動前ハウス

House for Seven People

TOKYO | 2013

024-

都心のワンルームマンションなどでの単身生活では、住居は寝に帰るだけのものになりがちである。核家族用の住宅と倉庫を他人同士の7人の共同生活のために再生させたこのプロジェクトでは、単身生活では得難い豊かな居住環境を、血縁にこだわらない集住というかたちを通して獲得しつつ、地域の人びととの関係も築き得る新しい家族のかたちが模索されている。

倉庫だった1階は大きなリビングに読み替え、解体時に発見された鉄扉を開放することで路地と地続きとなる。個室群のある2階は既存の窓を生かした周囲の廊下が縁側のような明るい空間となり、個室の向きと距離を調整している。既存のバルコニーにテントを架けた半屋外空間は、生活の気配を路地に染み出させる柔らかい縁となっている。血縁関係のない住人同士、住人と近隣の人、訪れる人が力まず自然に同居できるよう、縁の調整をすることによって、既存の建物がもっていた空間的特性と、新しい共同生活を相互に関係付け、新しい家族のかたちを支えている。

For single people living in studio apartments in the city, home tends to be a place where they only return to sleep. This project was designed to rejuvenate a house and storehouse originally made for a nuclear family in order to allow a group of seven unrelated people to live in a communal situation. While striving for a rich living environment – something that is often unavailable to people living alone – and making use of a collective living style without any need for family ties, the architects pursued a new type of family based on the relationship between local people.

The architects reinterpreted the first floor of the storehouse and turned it into a large living room. And by opening a steel door that had been discovered in the dismantling process, they created a space that adjoins the alley. On the second floor, containing several individual rooms, the existing windows in the surrounding corridor were used to make a bright verandah-like space, and to reorient and adjust the distance between the rooms. A semi-

築37年の既存住宅は、目黒川と山手通りに沿って中層のビルが建ち並び、低層の建物が内側に取り残された街区の細い路地に接していた。路地は幅が2m足らずで、法律上、新築や大規模な改修がほとんど不可能な敷地であった。

The existing house, built 37 years ago, abuts a narrow alley in a town where medium-rise buildings line the Meguro River and Yamate Street, but low-rise buildings still stand in the interior. As the alley has a width of less than two meters, legal restrictions make it nearly impossible to build a new structure or undertake a large renovation.

site plan 1:2500

鉄骨造の1階は大きな架構を生かし、前庭と地続きのリビングに。木造の2階は縁側アクセスの個室群。個室の壁が屋根まで達し、耐震性を担保している。リビングと個室群は前庭、外部階段、ベランダを介して繋がれている。

By making use of the large framework on the first floor of the steel construction, we made a front garden with an adjoining living room. The second floor, constructed out of wood, contains several individual rooms with access to the veranda. The walls of the rooms extend to the ceiling, ensuring greater earthquake resistance. The living room and the individual rooms are linked via the front garden, outside staircase, and verandah.

House for Seven People Mio Tsuneyama / mnm

026-

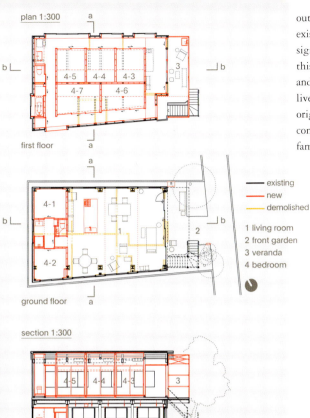

plan 1:300
first floor
ground floor
1 living room
2 front garden
3 veranda
4 bedroom

existing
new
demolished

section 1:300
b section
a section
elevation

outside space, made by draping a tent over the existing balcony, became a soft border zone, where signs of daily life exude into the alley. By adjusting this zone so that unrelated residents, residents and neighbors, and visitors have the ability to live together naturally, the spatial features of the original building become interrelated with this new communal lifestyle and support this new type of family.

インタビュー｜01｜常山未央

Q｜「en（縁）」というテーマについてどのように考えて参加されましたか？

「不動前ハウス」は7人の他人同士が住む家です。設計した当時は日本の状況に浦島太郎状態で、シェアして住むって海外では普通のことなのに、シェアハウスと名付けるなんて気張り過ぎだろう、と思っていました。住むってことは、他人とだろうが、家族とだろうがそんなに変わらない。もっと住むこと自体を建築がどう支えられるかを考えました。目黒駅から徒歩10分の都心に近く、川と山手通り、東急目黒線という大きなインフラに囲まれた環境で、どう人と豊かに共存できるか。どう家族や同居人の存在を感じながら、それぞれの生活を成り立たせるか。どう安心感を保ちながら、ざっくばらんに近所の人と接することができるか。

それは「縁」の建築でいう、「ふち」をうまく調整することだったように今は思います。個室と廊下、廊下とベランダ、ベランダとリビング、リビングと路地。

「不動前ハウス」はリビングと個室群が屋外階段で繋がれています。新築だと不便なので積極的には外部に階段はつくらないと思いますが、既存がたまたまそうであるので、仕方ないか、という判断になります。既存のもつ特性のおかげで一度外に出る動線が家の中に生まれ、外と中の「ふち」がファジーになり、家の生活が必然的に外へ染み出して行きます。すでに存在する建物（モノ）と現在の人の営みのたまたまの繋がりが、図らずも地域まで巻き込んでしまう。そういうたまたまを

路地に開けた大きなリビングは、家に属することで個人的要求にも対応しながら、多くの人を許容することで、よりパブリックな性格をもっている。鉄扉やカーテンの開閉により、用途に応じて路地との関係を調整し、分割できる。

The large living room, which opens onto the alley, responds to individual needs as part of the house, and by accommodating many people, it also possesses a more public character. By opening or closing the iron door or curtain, it is possible to change or divide the relationship with the alley depending on the situation.

解体時に出てきた鉄扉はかつて倉庫だった時に使われていたもので、そのまま利用した。既存の建物を資源として引き受け、新しい使い方に対応させながら、次の数十年に繋がるよう、硬い骨格は他の用途を見据え、建具やカーテン、テントなどの柔らかいものが現在の生活を支えている。

An iron door that surfaced in the process of dismantling the house had once been used for a storehouse, so we decided to use it just as it was. While accepting the existing house as a resource and adapting it for new uses, we anticipated that the hard framework would be used in other ways, creating a link to the next few decades. We also anticipated that the soft elements, such as fixtures, curtains, and tents, would provide support for the residents' present lifestyle.

House for Seven People   Mio Tsuneyama / mnm

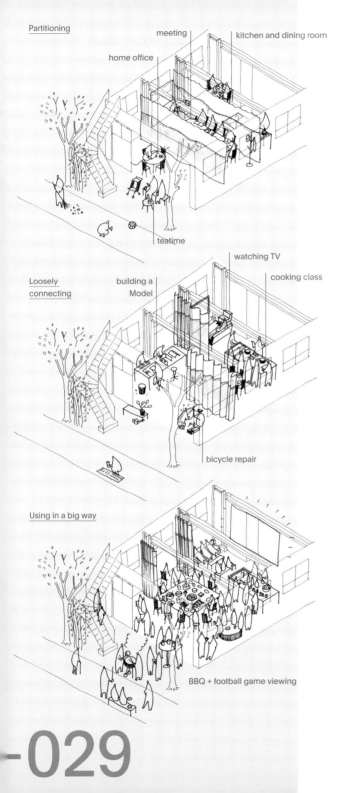

Partitioning
home office
meeting
kitchen and dining room
teatime

Loosely connecting
building a Model
watching TV
cooking class
bicycle repair

Using in a big way
BBQ + football game viewing

「縁」という言葉で許容してしまう緩さが日本の街にはあり、それが思いがけなく生活を楽しくしているように思います。

当初、アーティストやクリエイターなど、大きなリビングを生かせる人に住んでもらえれば、と思っていました。しかし現在はベンチャー企業に勤める女性や、大使館に勤める人も住んでいます。そういった、ちょっとハイソな人たちが、工場のようながらんとした鉄骨むき出しのリビングで、寒い中ダウンジャケットを着こみ、ブーツを履きながら料理をしたり、雨の中、屋外階段を上下している様子を見ると、これまでの価値観とは異なる住み方をしているように思います。「不動前ハウス」の家賃は周辺のワンルームマンションとさほど変わりません。もっと安い金額で同じ地域に住むことも可能だと思います。住むことに対する価値観を変えたのは、「人の縁」「モノの縁」「地域の縁」から成る、楽しく緩い生活を支える、建築への信頼のように思います。

Interview | 01 | Mio Tsuneyama

Q | How did you approach the theme of *en* in this exhibition?

This is a house occupied by seven unrelated people. At the time we designed it, it was seen as something unbelievable in Japan. Although shared living was a regular thing in other countries, it seemed extravagant to call it a "shared house." But whether it's with other people or your own family, daily life isn't really that different. I thought more about how architecture could provide support for people's lives. How could people live a rich life together in an environment that was surrounded by large infrastructure like a river, Yamate Street, and the Tokyu Meguro train line near central Tokyo, about a ten-minute walk from Meguro Station? How shape would people's lives take as they sensed the presence of family members or other residents? While maintaining a sense of security, how could they relate in an open way with the neighbors?

2階はもともと和室の続き間であり、その奥行きを引き継ぐよう、ぐるっと外壁に沿って縁側のような廊下を設けられている。そこから個室へ光と風を採り、アクセスする。個室のモノが明るい廊下へと溢れ出し、廊下で過ごす時間を延長している。

既存の窓が並ぶ廊下は、その形状や大きさ、位置から、かつての生活の様子を伝えている。住む人の意識が建物のもつ時間に接続し、生活を支える家そのものへの愛着を生んでいる。

既存のベランダにテントを張った半屋外空間は、個室群へのエントランス兼小さなリビングである。テントで覆うことでパジャマでも過ごせる場所となり、中での営みと路地の往来の気配を相互に感じながら、両者が心地よく共存できる。

The second floor was originally a series of Japanese-style rooms, so we preserved the original depth and made a veranda-like corridor, which continues along the exterior wall. This allowed light and wind inside the rooms and also provided greater access to them. The things inside the rooms overflow into the bright corridor, increasing the amount of time people spend there.
The shape, size, and position of the preexisting windows that line the corridor convey a sense of the life that was once lived there. The residents' awareness connects to the time contained in the building, creating a fondness for the house, which supports their daily life.
The semi-outdoor space, with a tent installed in the preexisting veranda, functions as both an entrance to the individual rooms and a small living room. Since it is covered with the tent, residents can spend time there in their pajamas, and while quietly conveying the fact that they are doing something there or coming and going through the alley, everyone can live together in a comfortable way.

House for Seven People Mio Tsuneyama mnm

030

Thinking back on it now, it seems as if I successfully adjusted the *fuchi* (edges) in this example of *en* architecture, making connections between the individual rooms and corridor, the corridor and the veranda, the veranda and the living room, and the living room and the alley.

In this house, the living room and the individual rooms are linked by an exterior staircase. In a new building, it would be too inconvenient to build a staircase outside, but because the original structure happened to be that way, I decided there was no choice but to accept the situation. Thanks to the existing characteristics of the structure, a flow line leading outside was created in the house, and through a fusion of outside and inside edges, it was inevitable that life there would spill outside. The link that happened to be created between the existing building (object) and the current residents' activities unexpectedly became involved with the local area. In Japanese cities, there is a looseness, a kind of accidental occurrence that might called *en*, which unexpectedly makes life enjoyable.

Initially, I envisioned residents like artists and creators, who would make the most of the big living room. But now there is a woman who works at a venture business and a man who works at an embassy living there. Watching people from a slightly higher social background cooking in down jackets and boots in cold weather in the cavernous living room, with an exposed steel frame that recalls a factory, and walking up and down the outside staircase in the rain, it seems as if their lives are based on different values from those of the past. The rent is roughly the same as it would be for a studio apartment in the neighborhood. I think you could live in the same area for less money. I believe that the reason I was able to affect people's values in regard to their way of living was due to their trust in architecture, which supports an enjoyable, loose life that arises from *en* between people, things, and the local area.

最小限の広さの個室は、高さを目一杯に使い、開放感を獲得。現しにした小屋組と素地の壁は、白い共用部と対比される。個室の領域が明快になり、建具やカーテンを開け広げても、安心して過ごせる。

In the smallest room, we made full use of the height to create a sense of openness. The exposed roof truss and wall surface create a contrast with the common white parts. By clearly marking the territory in the individual rooms, residents can relax there even when the fittings or curtains are open.

日常と地続きの出来事をつくり、
居場所のように人を繋げる

Creating Events
alongside Daily Life
to Form Links Between People

西田司＋中川エリカ

Osamu Nishida＋Erika Nakagawa

ヨコハマアパートメント

Yokohama Apartments

YOKOHAMA | 2009

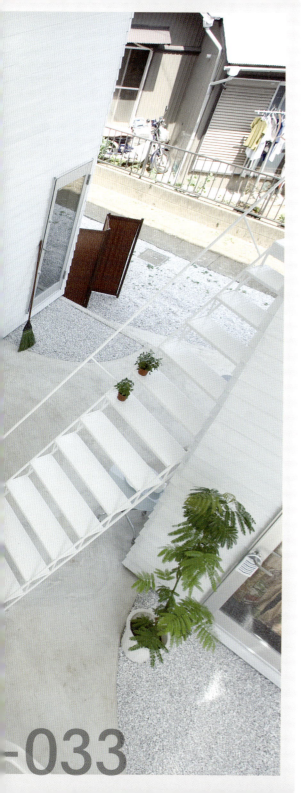

敷地は交通の便が悪く、新たに引っ越してくる人も少ない高齢化の進む街にある。また、周囲の土地は高低差が大きく、木造家屋が密集して建っている。全4戸のこの集合住宅は、こうした場所に、若い人が生き生きと居住や制作、展示を行う木造賃貸アパートとして計画された。4本の三角の壁柱で高く持ち上げられた個室群の下に「広場」と呼ばれる半屋外の共有空間がある。四方に大きな開口をもつオープンな建ち方であり、街への風通しを良くしている。壁柱の回りに各住戸へアクセスする階段、壁柱の中に専用の倉庫があり、それぞれの所有物や生活の一部が広場に溢れ出てくる。居住者が毎月1回、広場で行われるイベントなどの運営について話し合いを行っているが、住人以外のイベントを催すこともあり、他者を受け入れるコンパクトな公共空間となっている。建築を運営する小さな自治が根付きつつあり、活動は自走的である。

The lot is in an area without easy access to public transportation, and the town is home to an increasingly aging population and few new arrivals. In addition there is a huge difference in elevation between the lot and the surrounding area, densely packed with wooden houses. This apartment complex, containing a total of four units, was designed to provide wooden, rental housing where younger people could live, and make and display things in a vivid manner. Under a group of individual rooms, raised up with four, triangular pilasters, there is a semi-outside common area called the "open space." The open style of the building, with large openings on every side, provides good ventilation to the city. There is a staircase around the pilasters, providing access to each dwelling, and individual storage areas inside each of the pilasters, allowing the residents to store their possessions and allowing part of their lives to overflow into the open space. The residents hold meetings to organize monthly events in the space. Events involving other people are also held here, giving rise to a compact public space that accepts outsiders. A small association manages the building, and people are free to live spontaneously.

横浜市西戸部町は、道が狭くて高低差があり、街全体が立体交差する路地のような場所である。谷地なので、地面に近いほど暗く、空に近いほど明るい。この明らかに違うふたつの空間の質を断面的に活用し、4本の壁柱に高く持ち上げられたスラブの上に田の字型に仕切られた小屋が載るという構成が生まれた。

In Yokohama's Nishitobe-cho area, the streets are narrow and there are elevation differences, giving the entire town the feel of an alley with an overhead crossing. As the area is marsh land, the amount of darkness increases as you near the ground, and the amount of light increases as you near the sky. By making the most of these two distinct qualities in section, we created a structure containing four small huts divided into equal parts on a slab that is elevated with four wall pillars.

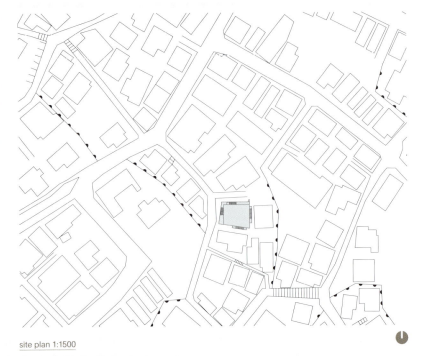

site plan 1:1500

スラブ下の広場は天井高5mの半外部である。半外部と外部の境界にあるのはビニルカーテン1枚だけであり、その物理的な境界の希薄さが、広場と街の境界も希薄にしている。ラフな空間に対し、居住者は自分自身でこの場所をどう使うかをあれこれ想起する。自発的だからこそ、アクションが連鎖して持続していく。境界の希薄さにより、そのアクションは広場内にとどまらず、近所にも波及していく。それはとても草の根的で微力だが、最も確実で強く、現代社会で取り扱うべきパブリックの姿である。

The square beneath the slab is a semi-outdoor area with five-meter-high ceilings. The only thing that divides the semi-outdoor space and the outside is a vinyl curtain, and the rarified nature of this physical border also imbues the border between the square and the town with a rarified quality. Despite this rough space, residents are free to use the area in any way that suits them. This element of spontaneity helps foster and sustain a chain of actions. Due to the rarified border, actions are not restricted to the square but extend into the surrounding neighborhood. Though this is a fairly small-scale, grass-roots approach, public forms should deal with contemporary society in the most confident and strongest way.

034-

Yokohama Apartments　Osamu Nishida + Erika Nakagawa

plan
1:200

1 open space
2 storage
3 common storage
4 private room
5 PS

first floor

ground floor

a section
1:200

インタビュー ｜ 02 ｜ 西田司＋中川エリカ

Q ｜「en（縁）」というテーマについてどのように考えて参加されましたか？

建築というのは、単にモノをつくるというのではなく、モノを通じて出来事もつくってしまうところがあります。「縁」という言葉にも、目に見えるモノだけではなく、目に見えない出来事をも含むニュアンスがあります。そして、「縁」という言葉が指す出来事は、非日常なアクシデントではなく、日常と地続きのドラマのように感じられます。身体的というか、実感ができる。経験的で、親密さがあります。

今回、「人の縁」というサブテーマをいただいていますが、壁のように人間を分けるのではなく、居場所のように人間を繋げる建築を表現したいと考えています。建築は、空間だけでなく、経済とか、コミュニティとか、社会の他の側面にもインパクトを与えます。建築をつくることは、どのような社会に向かいたいのか、人間の集まりはどうあるべきか、という方向付けをすることでもあります。

一方で、つくるということだけでなく、場を使う、建築を使っていく、ということにも、かなりの創造性があります。どのように生活したいか、生きたいかという価値観や欲望、決断の数々は、時に、家だけでなく、社会とのリンケージも含んでいるし、その一つひとつの選択の積み重ねで都市が出来ています。

だから、「ヨコハマアパートメント」に限らず、いつもそうなのですが、建築が、文化や習慣に訴えるようなインフラ、もしくは動力源にならないだろうかと期待しています。たとえ小さくても、インフラ的な役割をもつ建築は、時間に対する耐久性や持続性がある。街にとって、社会にとって、アンカーのような存在になります。小さなアンカーでも、コーディネーションの壮大さをもてば、都市への提言になるかもしれない。たくさんの複雑な問題を、ひとつの答えだけで鮮やかに解決することが難しい今だからこそ、チャレンジしたいのです。

日本館では、12組の建築家が、それぞれの建築

Yokohama Apartments Osamu Nishida + Erika Nakagawa

036-

を通じて、それぞれの「縁」を表現します。ひとつの空間に、同時に、ワッと異なる「縁」が集まるという状況は、それ自体が、多視点で、多中心で、とてもユニークだと思います。時代が変わろうと動き出す時、建築や、建築を表現するリプレゼンテーションも、変わるのかもしれません。こうなるべきだという結果、出口を共有するのではなく、「縁」というテーマ、入り口だけを共有して、12組の解釈やプロセスの自走性を大事にします。とてもオープンで、能動的な展覧会だと思っています。

Interview | 02 |
Osamu Nishida + Erika Nakagawa

Q | How did you approach the theme of *en* in this exhibition?

Architecture is not simply about making an object; it also contains an element of creating an event though that object. Similarly, the word *en* suggests not only visible things, but also invisible events. And the events that *en* suggests are not extraordinary accidents, but dramas that adjoin everyday life. In physical terms, it suggests something with a sense of reality, something experiential and intimate.

The exhibition's subtitle, the *en* of people makes me think about creating architecture that instead of dividing people like a wall, creates a place for them to be. Not only does architecture exert an impact on a space, it also affects other things, such as the economy, community, and society. Creating architecture is also informed by issues such as how to approach society and how people should gather.

On the other hand, it is not simply an act of creating something, there is a great deal of creativity involved in using a place and a building. Numerous values, desires, and decisions related to a particular type of lifestyle or way of living not only result in a house, but in some cases create a link with society, and this accumulation of individual choices also produces a city.

4本の壁柱を貫通する階段の踊り場は、4カ所それぞれで高さを変えている。広場を見下ろすステージであり、街と広場／広場と個室の立体的なバッファーでもある。この建築では、水回りと寝室のみをおのおのの専有、それ以外はエネルギーを含め、全部共有としている。結果、大部分が共有とはいえ、居住者は使用可能な空間をより多くもっており、広場は、自分の場所でもあるけれど、自分ではない人の場所でもある。だから、特にイベントがない日常的な日でも、何が起こるかは不確定である。街と地続きで、見る角度によって異なる表情を見せる。

The staircase landing, which penetrates the wall pillars, creates a different height in each of the four places. It is a stage to look down over the square, and a three-dimensional buffer between the town and square, and the square and the individual rooms. In this building, only the wet areas and bedrooms are completely private areas; everything else, including energy, is shared by all of the people. As a result, despite the fact that the majority of the building is shared, this provides the residents with more useable spaces, and the square belongs both to each individual person and everyone at the same time. Thus, anything might happen there, especially on regular days when no events are planned. As it adjoins the town, the square displays a variety of features depending on how you look at it.

「ヨコハマアパートメント」は、生活の単位を圧倒的に変えることで、専有＜共有という逆転した所有バランスを提案し、人間が集まって住むことの本質を問うている。毎月1回、居住者会議を開いて、この建物の使い方を話し合い、そこに設計者も参加している。常にその場所のあり方を住民が考えることで、広場は人間とともに成長している。竣工して7年、持ち込み企画による公民館としても、居住者の試行による実験場としても、使われ続けている。居住者であるか否かは関係なく、人間は動かされ、出会い、発見し、生き生きと活動している。近所付き合いもSNS上での繋がりも同じ土俵で受け入れる、集まって住むための建築である。

By radically altering the unit of living, *Yokohama Apartments* proposes an inverted balance of ownership in which more weight is placed on the common than the private as a means of raising essential questions about the act of living together. In monthly meetings, the residents (as well as the designers) discuss how to use the building. By constantly considering the state of the place, the square evolves along with the people. Seven years after its completion, the building continues to be used both as a community center, where outside people can organize events, and a laboratory, where residents conduct various experiments. Regardless of whether one is a resident or not, people take part in lively activities, absorbing various influences, and encountering and discovering various things. Like neighborhood acquaintances or a social network system, the building is an arena for accepting each other and living together.

038–

Yokohama Apartments Osamu Nishida + Erika Nakagawa

In *Yokohama Apartments* as well as the rest of my work, I anticipate that architecture will serve as an infrastructure or a source of power that will appeal to a certain culture or behavior. Even if it only functions as a small form of infrastructure, architecture has a sense of durability and sustainability. It works as a kind of anchor in a town or society. Though it might only be a small anchor, if it includes a grand element of coordination, it can serve as a proposal to the city. In this era, in which it is difficult to arrive at a single answer or clear conclusion to many complicated problems, I feel it is more important than ever to take on new challenges.

Through their individual works, each of the 12 architects participating in this exhibition in the Japan Pavilion are expressing their own understanding of *en*. This situation, in which all different types of *en* are assembled in the same place at the same time, contains multiple viewpoints and focuses. It is a very unique approach. When an effort is made to change a given era, the way in which architecture is represented is also likely to change. This is not a conclusion that things should be a certain way or some kind of exit strategy. The theme of *en* provides us with an entrance, carefully respecting the autonomous nature of each architect's perspective and process. This promises to be a very open, proactive exhibition.

成瀬・猪熊建築設計事務所
Naruse Inokuma Architects

LT城西
LT Josai

NAGOYA | 2013

040–

血縁や地縁に
関係なく、
個が自由に繋がる
関係の構築

A Structure to Freely Trigger
Relationships between
Individuals without Blood or
Community Ties

かつて複数の世代から成り立っていた家族は、高度経済成長の中、地縁・血縁を断ち切った核家族という形式を経て、現在は人の動きがますます流動化し、ついに単身世帯が最も多い社会になってしまった。終身雇用も崩壊し、会社と核家族の時代が個(孤)の時代へと変化しつつあると言える。この状況を悲観的に捉えるのではなく「個が繋がる時代」として乗り越えるために、場づくりにおいてプログラム・運営と建築の両方が生まれ変わる必要がある。この作品は、こうした時代の新しい住まいの形として、新築で計画されたシェアハウスである。木造の慣習的なモジュールを用いながら2間(3.6m)のグリッドに13の個室を立体的に配し、建物の高さを2.5層分に調整することで複雑な凹凸をもつ立体的な空間が生まれている。共有のリビングやダイニング、アルコーブがひと繋がりになりながら分散しており、血縁関係にない人同士が集まって生活する家としてさまざまな使い方と距離感が生み出されている。

During the period of high-economic growth, Japanese families, which in the past were composed of multiple generations, became nuclear families, severing ties with people in the local community as well as blood relatives. This led to the contemporary state in which people's movements are increasingly fluid and a society with a higher number of single-person households. The lifetime employment system has also collapsed, and the age of society and family seems to be moving into an age of the individual (solitude).

Rather than viewing this with pessimism, it is necessary to make changes in the programming, management, and architecture of places to enter an age in which individuals are linked. This work, a new form of dwelling for such an age, was designed as a newly constructed, shared house. While making use of the customary wooden model, 13 rooms are arranged three-dimensionally on a 3.6-meter grid. By adjusting the height of the building to the scale of 2.5 floors, the architects arrived at a three-dimensional space imbued with a complex uneven quality. And through the common living room, dining room, and alcove are connected, they are

plan 1:300

1 living room
2 dining room
3 kitchen
4 private room
5 lavatory
6 entrance
7 lighting room
8 roof terrace
9 courtyard
10 car parking
11 bicycle parking
12 drying area
13 restroom

単純なグリッドを採用した平面。南北両方の採光を考え、北にも広く庭を確保している。入居者は家庭菜園などを自由に楽しむことができる。

The floor plan makes use of a simple grid. After considering the amount of light on both the north and south sides, we decided to create an expansive garden on the north side. This allows the residents to enjoy making a kitchen garden.

site plan / ground floor

mezzanine floor

中間層を挟むことで、複雑な断面を生み出している。

Inserting the space between neutral levels creates a complex section.

first floor

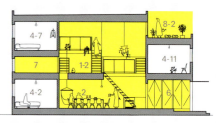

a section 1:300

042-

LT Josai   Naruse Inokuma Architects

dispersed, facilitating a variety of uses and a sense of distance in a house where people who are not related by birth can assemble and live.

インタビュー│03│成瀬友梨＋猪熊純

Q│「en（縁）」というテーマについてどのように考えて参加されましたか？

私たちは、建築をつくる時に時代性を形にすることを考えます。たとえばこの「LT城西」は、人と人との関係において今日らしい住空間の構成を、建築によって成立させようと試みたものです。

戦前、地域とともに日常の生活が営まれていた日本は、戦後の高度経済成長の中、郊外に住みながら父親が都心に勤めるというライフスタイルが確立し、核家族と会社という単純なコミュニティ形式が成立しました。現在は人の動きが流動化するとともに高齢化が進み、家は単身世帯が最も多くなった一方で、会社も終身雇用が崩壊し、コミュニティ単位は「個（孤）」という時代へと突入しつつあります。

私たちは、こうした状況を悲観的に捉えるのではなく、いったん「個」に還元された状態から、血縁や地縁にも関係なく自由に繋がる、新しい関係の構築に興味があります。過去の農村的な繋がりを懐かしむのではなく、個人同士から繋がるからこそできるような、多様で幸せな社会を目指すことが、私たちの世界観です。

こうした、これからの時代らしい人のかかわり方に、どのような言葉を当てはめることができるか、私たちはここ数年ずっと模索してきました。「シェア」という言葉は比較的最近になって人の関係性に対して使われ始めたために固定したイメージが少なく、積極的に使っているのですが、イメージが固定されていないがゆえに、分かりにくさもあります。

今回設定されたテーマ「縁」はそうした中で、私たちにとって、とてもしっくりくる言葉でした。地縁といった、古いコミュニティも含んでいながら、同時に一期一会の出会いのような意味も含みます。古

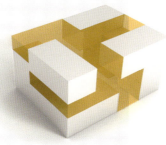

private space

白が個室、黄色が共用スペースを示す。プライベートな個室を立体的に組み合わせた残りの空間が共用スペースになっている。共用空間は、凹凸のある複雑な形をしている。

The white areas denote individual rooms, and the yellow ones are common spaces. By combining the private rooms three-dimensionally, the remaining areas become common spaces. These spaces have uneven, complex shapes.

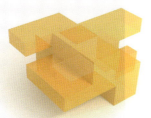

integration

common space

道路側のアノニマスな外観。
The anonymous exterior on the roadside.

1

2

1｜キッチン前の溜まりから奥のソファコーナーを望む。奥に見える階段は、1階と2階を、手前に見える階段は2階と2.5階を繋ぐ。複数の居場所が点在する。
2｜ソファコーナーからダイニングを望む。1階、2階それぞれに複数の居場所が存在する。
3｜エントランスから共用スペースを望む。水平・垂直両方向に広がりのある空間。個室のドアは直接共用スペースに面さないようになっており、プライバシーの高い構成としている。

3

LT Josai｜Naruse Inokuma Architects

4｜入居者に人気のソファコーナー。窓辺で明るい、アルコーブ状の空間。
5｜ダイニングは天井高を抑えた落ち着いた空間。

1｜View of sofa corner in the rear from the gathering spot in front of the kitchen. The staircase visible in the back connects the first and second floor, and the one in the foreground runs between the second and 2.5 floor. Various living places are scattered around the space.
2｜View of dining area from the sofa corner. The first and second floors contain a variety of living places.
3｜View of common space from the entrance. The space extends in both a horizontal and vertical direction. Designed so that the doors to individual rooms do not directly abut the common spaces, the structure ensures a maximum of privacy.
4｜Residents gather in the popular sofa corner. The alcove-like space is bright alongside the windows.
5｜The dining area is a relaxed space with a restricted ceiling height.

くから使われる言葉であると同時に、私たちが今の日本に必要だと考えてきた「個が自由に繋がる」関係にも近いように思えました。今回の展覧会は、同時代の建築家の作品が複数集まることで、現代的な縁とは何なのかということを、あぶり出すような場になるのではないかという気がしています。

Interview｜03｜Yuri Naruse ＋ Jun Inokuma

Q｜How did you approach the theme of *en* in this exhibition?

When we make a building, we think about how to shape to the distinctive qualities of our times. For example, *LT Josai* was an attempt to use architecture to create a living space with contemporary sensibilities based on relationships between people.

In pre-war Japan, everyday life was conducted in correspondence to the local area. Then in the midst of rapid postwar economic growth, a lifestyle in which the family lived in the suburbs and the father worked in the heart of the city took hold, and a simple form of community based on the nuclear family and society was established. Today, while working styles have grown more fluid, Japan is faced with an aging population, single-person households have reached an all-time high, and at the same time, the lifetime employment system has collapsed and we have been plunged into an age in which the basic community unit is the individual (i.e., a state of solitude).

Instead of viewing this situation with pessimism, we are interested in creating new relationships in which individuals can freely form connections without any blood ties or direct links to the local community. Without a sense of nostalgia for the connections that existed in farming villages of the past, our worldview is based on the idea of realizing a diverse, happy society where it is possible to form links between individuals.

For the last few years, we have continually

1 | 2階の共用スペース。複数の小さな階段を利用して個室にアクセスする。それぞれの階段からはひとつかふたつの個室にアクセスでき、共用部との距離感を取るのに役立つ。2階のリビングは山の中腹の中継地点のような場。
2 | 個室の内部。半層ずれているので、個室も天井の高さにバリエーションがある。
3 | 共用部はすべて大きく繋がっていながら、互いに見えないところもたくさんある。全体として、高さや広がりに違いのある場が、連続的に繋がるような空間である。
4 | 北側の庭でバーベキューを楽しむ入居者たち。

1 | Common space on the second floor. Individual rooms can be accessed by several small staircases. Each provides access to one or two rooms, a useful way of creating a sense of distance from the common space. The living room on the second floor recalls a staging point halfway up a mountain.
2 | Interior of individual rooms. As there is a half-floor difference between rooms, the ceiling height varies from one to the next.
3 | While all of the common sections are largely connected, there are also many places where the view between them is obstructed. Though the overall space has places with different heights and widths, it is a space that is continuously linked.
4 | Residents enjoying a barbecue in the garden on the north side of the building.

LT Josai   Naruse Inokuma Architects

046-

en: art of nexus

searched for a word that could be applied to the way that people will relate to each other in the future. The word "share" has been adopted relatively recently in regard to human relations, and since it is largely free of fixed images, we have been making use of it. On the other hand, the lack of fixed images also means that the term is rather unclear.

With this in mind, the theme of en in this exhibition struck us as an ideal term. While suggesting a connection to the local area and old community, it also suggests one-of-a-kind encounters. And though it is a word that has been used for centuries, it seems like an apt way to describe relationships in which individuals form links freely – something that we believe is essential in Japan. By assembling a group of works by architects who active in the same era, this exhibition promises to shed light on the nature of contemporary *en*.

3

4

Padiglione Giappone Biennale Architettura 2016

-047

A Space and Links between People Inspired by Small Economies

「小さな経済」への気づきが生んだ空間、そして人と人との繋がり

仲建築設計スタジオ
Naka Architects' Studio

食堂付きアパート
Apartments with a Small Restaurant

TOKYO | 2014

048

近代化の過程で一般化した「専用住宅」は個人の生活を分割し、プライバシーを偏重することで、都市生活を硬直化させてきた。

「食堂付きアパート」は、個人の生業による「小さな経済」に着目し、地域に開かれた生活環境をつくろうとしている。小さな経済は情報技術の発達により新しい形で顕在化しつつあり、そこには、他者の存在や自己承認に対する期待が含まれている。

敷地は東京の下町で、職住一体の生活スタイルが根付く商店街に近接する。5つのSOHO住戸、食堂、シェアオフィスを、半屋外の「立体路地」が繋いでいる。この立体路地は共用廊下と各戸のテラスを合わせた幅3mほどの縁であり、木造密集地域の路地を螺旋状に展開させている。立体路地は近隣と住戸の間、食堂は街路と建築の間、仕事場は寝室と立体路地の間に位置する。結果として、プライベートな空間から街までが、相互浸透的な中間領域を孕みながら連続し、内発的で都市的なかかわり合いが生まれている。

Houses made exclusively for living, a concept which took hold as part of the modernization process, divided people's lives and by placing a strong emphasis on privacy, led to increased rigidity in urban life.

Apartments with a Small Restaurant focuses on the small economy of individual livelihoods and attempts to create a living environment that is open to the surrounding area. While new types of small economies are being realized through the development of information technology, they also contain certain expectations regarding the existence of others and self-recognition.

Built on a lot in Tokyo's old town, the work promotes a lifestyle of living and working in the same place, a tradition rooted in the nearby shopping arcade. The work connects five *soho* (small office, home office) living units, a dining hall, and a shared office space to a semi-outdoor, three-

site plan 1:1500

敷地はちょうど商業地域と住宅地域の境界に位置する。近傍が木造密集地域であることから、近年、道路の拡幅や建物の不燃化に対する建て替え助成などにより、街が大きく変わろうとしている。こうしたことから新旧の住民が交流できるような集合住宅が求められた。

The lot is situated right on the border between a business district and a residential area. As the neighborhood has been designated as a densely populated area of wooden structures, government subsidies to widen the roads and fireproof buildings have led to drastic changes in the town. Based on these things, we felt the need for an apartment building that would foster exchanges between old and new residents.

section 1:300

1 shared office
2 small restaurant
3 studio
4 bedroom
5 alley

「小さな経済」にまつわる用途、すなわち、SOHO住戸、食堂、シェアオフィスを複合させた建築である。街路レベルから3階まで、各住戸の玄関前テラスと一体になった共用廊下——「路地」と名付けた——が、螺旋状に展開する。立体路地は、階によってその雰囲気が異なる。1階は隣家に囲まれ薄暗く、2階では隣家のバルコニーと向き合い、そして3階は隣家の屋根の高さにあって開放的である。

Based on the concept of small economies, this complex building includes *soho* (small office, home office) living units, and a shared office space. A spiral-shaped common corridor – or as we call it, "alley" – extends from street level to the third floor and is integrated with a terrace that runs in front of each apartment's entrance. This three-dimensional alley gives rise to a different atmosphere on each floor. The first floor is rather dark because it is surrounded by other houses, the second floor faces the balcony of a neighboring house, and the third floor is open and has the same height as the roof of the house next door.

Apartments with a Small Restaurant   Naka Architects' Studio

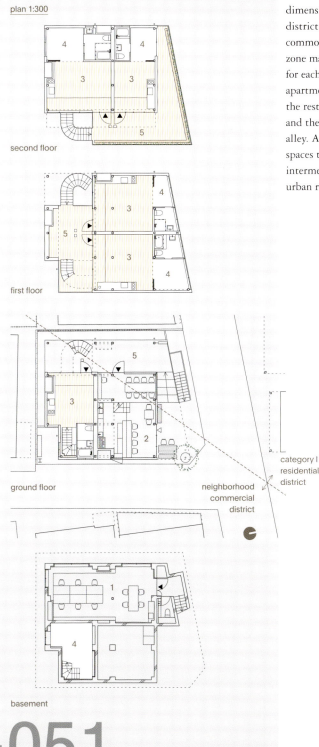

plan 1:300

second floor

first floor

ground floor

category I residential district

neighborhood commercial district

basement

dimensional alley. Located in a densely-populated district of wooden buildings, the spiral-shaped common alley is a roughly three-meter-wide border zone made up of a common corridor and terraces for each unit. The alley is positioned between the apartments and the surrounding neighborhood, the restaurant between the street and the building, and the work area between the bedroom and the alley. As a result, everything from the privates spaces to the town are linked in an interpenetrative, intermediate range, giving rise to a spontaneous, urban relationship.

インタビュー│04│仲建築設計スタジオ

Q│「en（縁）」というテーマについてどのように考えて参加されましたか？

「縁」という漢字は、両義的な言葉だと思いました。一般的には「関係」という意味をまず思い浮かべますが、何かと何かの「間（あいだ）」に起こることを指しますよね。一方で、「縁」をあえて「ふち」と読むと、「はじ、へり」を指すように思いました。そのため、「縁」という漢字から、空間性をもった境界のようなことをイメージしました。

私たちが展示する「食堂付きアパート」は、食堂やシェアオフィスが複合した集合住宅です。複数の用途の境界面を操作し、相互浸透的な中間的な領域をもつような建築です。たとえば、住宅のプライベートな空間と外部の共用廊下の間にはスタジオと名付けた空間がありますが、このスタジオは内部と外部の境界が空間化されたものと言えます。あるいはまた、集合住宅と街路の間には食堂がありますが、ふたつの領域が混じり合うことを意図して設計した空間です。このようにしてつくられる集合住宅は、街路からプライベートな空間までが厚みのある空間を介しながら繋がっていきます。

なぜそのような設計をしたのか。それは、「小さな経済」に着目したからです。個人の生業——仕事や商売——はもちろん、趣味や特技を多少の対価をもって交換し合うような活動に着目して、「小さな経済」と表現しています。たまたま敷地が東京の下町にあり、職住一体の生活スタイルが根

soho living unit

- Alley: The alley could be used for a sign or as a recreation spot.
- Studio: The studio is large, making it easy to lay things out.
- Private space: Positioned in the rear, the bright private space abuts the outside. The fittings can be arranged to partition this space and the studio.

Apartments with a Small Restaurant   Naka Architects' Studio

052-

スタジオは居住者の「小さな経済」のための空間である。プライベートな空間と外部の中間に位置し、仕事場や趣味の部屋として使われている。

スタジオの外側は「路地」である。一見すると幅3ｍの空間に見えるが、玄関前テラスと共用廊下を一体化したものである。屋根付きの空間であるためいろいろな使い方が可能である。

路地に沿って共用のファシリティが配置されているが、特に、食堂は路地の始まりの位置にある。食堂は集合住宅と街の双方に対して開かれた、中間的な領域となっている。

The studio is a space designed to enhance the residents' small economies. Positioned between a private space and the outside, it is used both as a work and play room. The alley is outside the studio. Though it appears to be three meters wide, the space is integrated with the entrance terrace and common corridor. And as it is covered with a roof, the space facilitates many different uses. Though various shared facilities line the street, the restaurant is positioned at the beginning of the alley. The restaurant is open to both the apartments and the town, creating an intermediary space.

付いている地域だったということもありますが、一方で、情報技術の進展によっていろいろな働き方や趣味の共有の仕方が生まれているような世相もあります。実際に私たちの事務所ではいろいろな事例を採集していますが、実にいろいろな個人ベースの、小さな経済活動がある。そしてそれが、無理のない、持続的な繋がりや気遣いといったものを生み出していることに気が付きました。

経済活動というのは相手や外部を必要とします。このような状況において、プライバシーの確保のみが住宅をつくる原動力になるのか疑問でした。ですので、「食堂付きアパート」は、近代以降連綿とつくられ続けてきた、「専用住宅」に対する批判でもあります。専用住宅という前提を維持したままでは、繋がり──縁（en）──というものは生まれないと思っています。住むことと働くことを切り分けずに、個人のみずみずしい生活をそのまますくい取るような生活環境をつくることができないか。「小さな経済」に対する気づきが、先に述べたような設計に繋がっていきました。

Interview | 04 | Naka Architects' Studio

Q | How did you approach the theme of *en* in this exhibition?

The word *en*, written with the *kanji* character "縁," strikes me as an ambiguous term. The first meaning that usually comes to mind is "connection," but we might also use it to mean a "space" that arises between two things. Or by reading the character *fuchi* rather than *en*, we are reminded of a "rim" or "edge." Based on this, we might imagine something like a border imbued with a spatial quality.

The work we are displaying, *Apartments with a Small Restaurant*, is an apartment complex with a restaurant and shared office space. By manipulating the surface of the border with multiple applications, we created a building that contains interpenetrative, intermediate areas. For example, between the private living spaces and a common exterior corridor,

diagram of three-dimensional alley

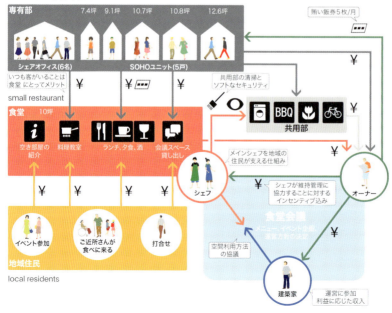

「小さな経済」ダイアグラム：SOHO住戸と食堂がさらに地域の住民とも繋がりながら行われる小さな経済活動の仕組みを図で示したもの。

Small economies: This diagram shows the structure of small economic activities, which create links with the soho (small office, home office) living units and dining hall as well as with people in the area.

Apartments with a Small Restaurant　Naka Architects' Studio

054–

食堂は、街路側とアパート側のふたつの入り口をもち、性格の異なるふたつのスペースをもつ。食堂の大きさは10坪と小さいが、それはオーナーによる独自運営を可能にしている。シェフが建物全体の維持管理にも貢献するようにしたり、SOHO居住者やシェアオフィス利用者が食堂を打ち合わせスペースに使えたり、用途複合の相乗効果もデザインしている。
プライベートな空間が地域社会にまで緩やかに繋がるような生活環境は、職住が混在した下町になじみながら、新しい交流の場所になりつつある。街並みが大きく変わるこの地域のために、住宅のつくり方を通して貢献している。

The restaurant is equipped with two entrances, one on the street and the other on the apartment side, creating two spaces with different characters. Though the restaurant is small (ten-square meters), it can be run independently depending on the owner. As the chef assists with the maintenance and management of the entire building, residents of the *soho* units and users of the shared-office space can make use of the restaurant as a meeting space. The design sets out to realize a synergic effect through a multitude of uses.
The living environment, in which private spaces are loosely connected to the local community, recalls the old town area, which combines living and working spaces, and also functions as a place for new exchanges. The structure of the building makes a positive contribution to the neighborhood, where the cityscape is currently undergoing drastic changes.

there is a space we refer to a "studio." The border between the inside and outside of this studio is spatial. Or, for example, the restaurant is located between the apartments and the street in a space that was intentionally designed as a combination of the two areas. In this way, the apartments are both mediated by and linked to a wide area that extends from the street to the private spaces.

Why did we make this kind of design? This was the result of our focus on small economies. Naturally, this includes individual livelihoods (jobs, businesses), but also exchange-based activities with a certain degree of value, such as hobbies and special skills. The lot happened to be in Tokyo's old town, which is noted for a lifestyle of living and working in one place. On the other hand, current social conditions have given rise to a common approach to various kinds of work and play through the development of information technology. In fact, our own office houses many such examples as well as a wide range of individually-based, small economic activities. This led us to the realization that such a situation could create natural, sustained links and interests.

Economic activities require a client and an exterior. With this in mind, we questioned the motivation behind housing that is solely devoted to ensuring privacy. Thus, *Apartments with a Small Restaurant* is in part meant as a criticism of purely residential dwellings, which have continued to be built since the modern era. We believe that maintaining such a notion prevents connections (*en*) from arising. We thought it would be possible to create a living environment that directly resulted in a vibrant life for the individual without dividing the acts of living and working. Our awareness of small economies is linked to the design that we created.

The *En* of

House for Seven People Mio Tsuneyama / mnm
Yokohama Apartments Osamu Nishida + Erika Nakagawa
LT Josai Naruse Inokuma Architects
Apartments with a Small Restaurant Naka Architects' Studio
Guest House in Takaoka Nousaku Architects
House at Komazawa Park Mizuki Imamura + Isao Shinohara / miCo.
15A House Levi Architecture
Boundary Window Shingo Masuda + Katsuhisa Otsubo Architects
The Floor of Atsumi, etc. 403architecture [dajiba]
House in Chofu Koji Aoki Architects
Projects in Kamiyama BUS
Umaki Camp Beat Shrine dot architects

Things

消費社会論の時代において、「モノ」は、意味作用の領域に属するものと見なされていた。いずれもが、物理的な水準から自立した意味作用の水準で流通し消費されることでのみ、意味あるものとして承認された。そこで価値とされたのは、新奇性であった。大衆的な注目を浴びるものが価値あるものとされ、メディアに流通する。

ところが2010年代辺りから、建築家は、意味作用には属さない「モノ」の側面にあらためて着目するようになる。つまり、物質性である。「モノ」の質感、時間性、身体との交わり、ふるまいの起こる場への感触に着目するようになる。そして「モノ」の物質性への関心の高まりは、建築家が自らの身体性を発見することと連動している。建築家は、抽象的な図面の世界から抜け出し、建築が成り立つ場の現実性と素直に向き合っていく。場所の雰囲気、改築されることになる家の質感、使われる素材の手触り、住むことになる人びとの実生活を、観察し、対話し、聴いて、見て、嗅ぐといった身体的な過程を通じて解釈していく。

さらに、「モノ」の建築家たちは、建築がつくり出される過程にも関心を向ける。能作文徳は述べている。「建築はモノの集合によってできている。建築は分業化された複数のモノを組み合わせる協同作業である。分業化によって部材や製品には固有の履歴とプロセスが生じる。つまりさまざまなモノや人といったアクターを関係づけるネットワークが形成される」。建築は、「モノ」の集合として捉えられる。「モノ」

を集合させ、組み合わせ、形にしていくさまざまな人間が、建築にかかわってくる。人間と「モノ」を構成要素とする行為者の集合体が成り立ってくる。建築は、「モノ」と人間が集合し相互連関していくところにおいて立ち現れる形として把握される。

そして、「モノ」の建築家たちは、用途変更や家族構成の変化に対し、床面積や建築エレメントを減じることで対応する。つまり減築である。減築が、新しい質をもつ空間をつくり出す。

「モノ」は、複数の「モノ」として捉えられる。「調布の家」にも見られるように、「モノ」のおのおのは、多様な時間性をたたえた個物である。複数の「モノ」は、それが新奇であれ、古いものであれ、等価なものとみなされる。独特の質感をもつのであれば、「モノ」は価値あるものとされ、建築の要素になる。個物の存在感は、「モノ」の質感、雰囲気として生じる。建築家たちは、おのおのの個物の支えとなる時間の固有性、懐かしさと向き合い、未来へと向かう時間性を新たにたたえた建築をつくり出していく。建築は、「モノ」を連関させ、網の目状の組織へと織り成していくこととして、再定義されている。 [MS]

Back when the consumer society was a subject of theoretical discussion, the "thing" was regarded as belonging to the domain of signification. In any case, things are recognized as having meaning for being distributed and consumed at the level of signification, independent from the physical level. What was valued in that context was novelty. Things that attracted mass interest were seen as having value and were widely covered in the media.

From about 2010 on, however, architects have paid new attention to an aspect of "things" that is not associated with signification: their materiality. They began to focus on the texture, the touch of things, their temporality, their interactions with the body, and the feel of the place where interactions with them occur. That rising interest in the materiality of things is connected to architects' discovering their own physicality. Architects are breaking out of the abstract world of plans and honestly facing the reality of the place where a building will rise. The ambience of the site, the feel of house to be rebuilt, the touch of the materials used, the actual lifestyles of the people who will live there: architects are learning about them through the physical processes of observation, conversation, listening, looking, and smelling.

In addition, architects of "things" are interested in the process by which a building is built. Fuminori Nousaku said, "A building comes about through an assemblage of things. Architecture takes teamwork, combining many things produced through a division of labor. Through that division of labor, each of the parts and products has its own history

and processes. That is, a network connecting a variety of things and people as actors is formed." Architecture can be regarded as an assemblage of things. And many different people are involved in architecture, bringing things together, combining them, making forms. An assemblage bade of actors, in which both humans and things are components, is formed. A building is grasped as a form that appears through interactions as people and things are brought together.

Moreover, architects of "things" may respond to usage changes and changes in family composition by reducing floor space and architectural elements, by rebuilding in a smaller form. That shrinkage creates spaces with new qualities.

In this approach, "things" are treated as multiples. As we can see in the "House in Chofu," the various "things" are separate objects with a great variety of temporality. Some are new and novel, some are old, some are regarded as equivalents. If it has a distinctive texture or material quality, the "thing" is regarded as of value and becomes an element in the building. The presence of individual things arises from their textures, their atmospheres. Architects address the distinctiveness of the time period that underlies each of the individual things and the emotional attachments to each and creates a building newly filled with a future-oriented temporality. Architecture is redefined as connecting things and weaving together a mesh-like structure.   [MS]

Linking Memories and Townscape by Rearranging Things

モノの再配置によって
記憶を繋ぎ止め、
街並みと繋がる

能作アーキテクツ
Nousaku Architects

高岡のゲストハウス
Guest House in Takaoka
TOYAMA | 2016

これから人口のさらなる減少が見込まれる日本の田舎では、建物を新築・増築するよりも、古い建物を減築することで豊かな空間や暮らしを得られるのでないか——こうした認識を出発点として、この作品はまず日本建築がもっている木造の屋根の単位を生かして小さな3つの家に分解している。既存家屋の中央部分を解体することで、祖母の住まい、コモンダイニング、ゲストルームの間に中庭を設けて、家族以外のメンバーを受け入れる開かれたつくりにしている。さらに、解体の際に出てきたマテリアルを廃棄せずに、それらを建物の新たな資源として捉えてリユースした。取り外した瓦を葺き直すことで周りの風景や街並みと繋ぎ、既存の家屋に残されていた障子や欄間を残し、家族の生業であった銅器を計画に組み込むことで、家族の歴史や記憶を大切に保存している。屋根をクレーンで移設するダイナミックなモノの再配置には、お祭りのような祝祭性があり、また、その軽やかな可動性が、土地に深く根付いた古い建物に新たな息吹をもたらしている。

In the Japanese countryside, where the population is expected to decrease further in the future, it seemed best to reduce the size of an existing building instead making a new one or expanding an old one. With this idea as a starting point, the architects retained the wooden roof, a fundamental element in Japanese architecture, and divided the structure into three small houses. By dismantling the center of the original house, they created a living space for the grandmother, a common dining area, and an inner courtyard in the guest room. This design openly accepts people other than the family members.

Moreover, instead of disposing of the materials that emerged in the dismantling process, they were reused as a new building resource. By re-thatching the roofing tiles that were removed from the house, a link was created with the surrounding land- and townscape. And by retaining the *fusuma* (sliding paper doors) and transoms from the old house, and incorporating copper ware, the family's livelihood, into the plan, the work placed a special value on the family's history and memories. Rearranging

process of renovation

1. Dismantling the small buildings.

2. Expanding the kitchen and bathroom in the sitting room.

3. Our grandmother's living space after completion. Making the foundation for the dining room.

4. Erecting columns in the dining room.

5. Detaching the roof structure in the hipped roof.

6. Transferring the hipped roof to the dining room.

7. Dismantling the central volume, and covering the roof with existing tiles.

8. Finishing the dining room and guest room.

敷地は富山県高岡市。私たちが子供の頃まで過ごした場所である。既存の建物に祖母が住みながら少しずつ改修する計画。祖母の住まいの改修と水回りの増築を行った後、既存の小屋組をクレーンで移設して家屋の2階建て部分を解体する。移設した小屋組を新築した壁の上に載せて、客を招くコモンダイニングをつくる。瓦屋根に加えて、庭にある松や楓、灯籠、欄間、雪見障子や、この街の伝統産業の銅器などの既存のマテリアルを残しながら、3つの分棟に再配置する。

The site was in Takaoka, Toyama Prefecture. It was a place where we spent time as children. The plan called for the gradual renovation of our grandmother's house while she continued to live there. After renovating her living area and expanding the wet area, we used a crane to remove the existing roof structure and dismantle the second floor of the house. The roof structure was placed on a newly-built wall and used to create a common dining area for guests. In addition to the tiled roof, existing materials, such as the pine and maple trees in the garden, lanterns, *ramma*, *shoji* fitted with glass windows, and copper ware, a traditional industry in the town, were preserved and redistributed throughout the three wings.

plan 1:200

1 *tatami* room
2 kitchen
3 bedroom
4 dining room
5 guestroom
6 courtyard
7 grandmother's house

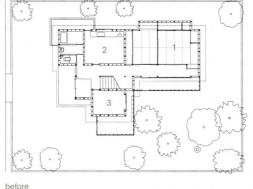
before

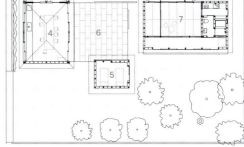
after

062-

Guest House in Takaoka   Nousaku Architects

things to coincide with the relocation of the roof (using a crane) gave the undertaking a festive quality, and this light sense of mobility also breathed new life into the old house, which was firmly rooted in the land.

インタビュー│05│能作アーキテクツ

Q│「en(縁)」というテーマについてどのように考えて参加されましたか？

「縁」という言葉は、現代的には「ネットワーク」と言い換えられるのではないかと思いました。ネットワークといっても、インターネット上の繋がりだけを意味するのではなくて、実際の「人」や「モノ」の連関のことだと思います。

「高岡のゲストハウス」の改修前の家屋に、私たちは子供の頃まで住んでいました。そこに残されたさまざまな「モノ」には家族の記憶や時間が内在しています。それを廃棄してしまうのか、それとも繋ぎ止めていくのか。周りの建物には瓦屋根が用いられていますが、そのような風景や街並みに対して、それを無視してしまうのか、繋がりを見出すのか。私たちはこの計画の中で「モノ」を通して具体的にそれらと連関できないかと思いました。

家族の記憶やありきたりな田舎の風景は、建築家の創作にとっては、邪魔なもの、あるいは格好のつかないウェットなものに捉えられるかもしれません。しかしそれらは、建築家だけではつくり上げることができないことに気づきました。こうした「モノ」の繋がりを考えることも「縁」なのではないかと思います。

ゲストハウスを一部に組み込んだのは、祖母が現在ひとり暮らしなので、家族や友人がその場所に訪れる機会を増やし、少しでも見守れるような状況をつくりたかったからです。分棟の形式にしたのは、ゲストハウスと祖母の住まいの距離を調整するためと、解体後にできた中庭が人の集まる場所になると期待したからです。そのような構成も人との「縁」と関係していると思います。

第1期工事で完成した祖母の住まい。雪見障子、木彫欄間、襖が再利用され、土間には庭で集めてきた小石が用いられた。天井は剥がされて小屋組が現しになり、家族によって壁の珪藻土(けいそうど)が塗られた。家に残された「モノ」を廃棄するのではなく、資源として捉えている。また建てることすべてを専門家に任せるのではなく、使う人たちも建てることにかかわってもらった。

Our grandmother's living area after the first stage of construction was completed. The window-equipped *shoji*, carved wooden transoms, and *fusuma* were reused and pebbles collected from the garden were used in the earthen floor. The ceiling indicated the removed wooden roof structure, and the diatomaceous earth was applied to the walls by the family. Rather than disposing of the things that were left in the house, we saw them as resources. Instead of leaving the building entirely up to professionals, we had the people who were going to live there become involved in the process.

Guest House in Takaoka Nousaku Architects

064-

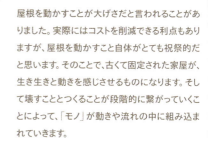

屋根を動かすことが大げさだと言われることがありました。実際にはコストを削減できる利点もありますが、屋根を動かすこと自体がとても祝祭的だと思います。そのことで、古くて固定された家屋が、生き生きと動きを感じさせるものになります。そして壊すこととつくることが段階的に繋がっていくことによって、「モノ」が動きや流れの中に組み込まれていきます。

「高岡のゲストハウス」のさまざまな「モノ」は最初は偶然そこに集められただけかもしれません。しかしそれらが時間をかけて存在してきたことが独特な質感に繋がっています。「縁」は偶然性を了解していくひとつの形式だと思います。偶然の出会いなどを「縁」という言葉を通して、私たちは自分自身が置かれた環境や、自分に起こる出来事を納得させていきます。私たちが生きている環境は偶然性に満ちていますが、その偶然の出会いの中で確かさをつくっていく。その「縁」の確かさを、物質化して支えていくことが建築の役割なのだと思います。

Interview | 05 | Nousaku Architects

Q | How did you approach the theme of *en* in this exhibition?

We thought that the word *en* could be rephrased using the contemporary term "network." This word does not only apply to the Internet but also to the connections between real people and things.

Before we renovated *Guest House in Takaoka*, we had lived there as children. The things that were there contained many family memories and times. We wondered whether we should dispose of them or make a connection to them. Though the surrounding buildings had roof tiles (*kawara*), we wondered if we should ignore that type of landscape or townscape or create a link to it. We finally decided that it would be possible to create concrete connections through these things in the project.

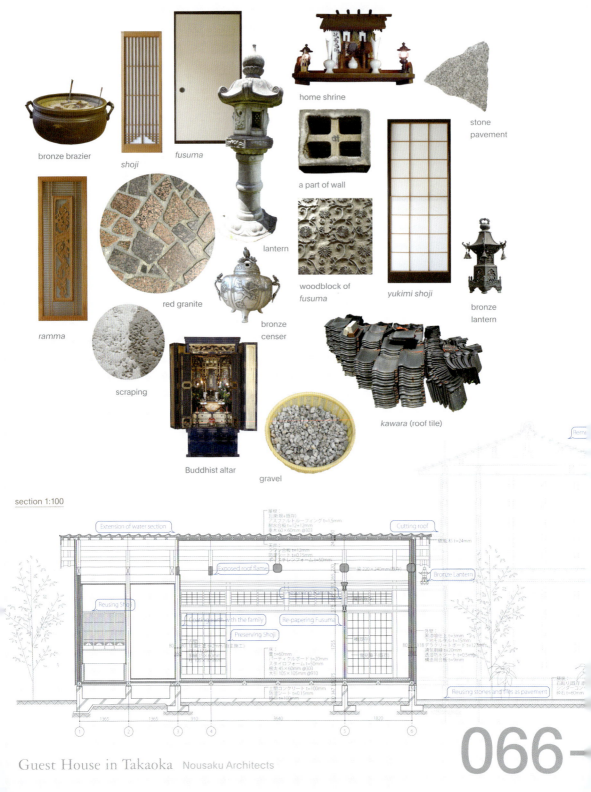

Guest House in Takaoka Nousaku Architects

建物は「モノ」の集合によってできている。「モノ」が配置されることで空間をかたちづくる。「空間」に重きを置くならば、「モノ」は空間を構成する単なる部品でしかないが、「モノ」に内在した時間やプロセスに着目するならば、「モノ」は能動的なアクターとしてストーリーを語り始める。移設された瓦屋根は地域の風景を、再利用された雪見障子や欄間は家族の記憶を、祖父母が製作した銅器は高岡の伝統産業を。このように「モノ」をアクターとして捉えるならば、建物を建てるということは、それぞれの「モノ」がもっているストーリーを相互に関係付けて組み立てることに似てくる。また、住みながら少しずつ建物をつくっていくことで、一度に全体を完成させるのでなく、既存の建物を解体して生じた部材を新しい建物で利用する。このような段階的な建設によって、修復しながら成長していくという「モノ」による新陳代謝のネットワークをつくり出そうとしている。

A building is made up of an aggregation of things. Distributing these things gives shape to the space. When a strong emphasis is placed on the space, things become little more than components that create the space. But if you focus on the time and process contained in the things, they function as actors that tell a story. The reinstalled roof tiles tell of the local landscape, the reused *shoji* and transoms tell of the family's memories, and the copper ware, made by our grandparents, tells of Takaoka's traditional industry. If we see things in this way, making a building is like creating a relationship and combining each of the stories contained in the things there. And by gradually making the building while grandmother is still living in it, you can dismantle the preexisting structure and use the components that emerged as a result in the new building without completing the whole thing all at once. Using this staged approach, we tried to create a metabolic network based on things that are reactivated as they mature.

Family memories and various rural landscapes could be seen as a hindrance or something unsightly in an architectural endeavor such as this. But we realized that the architect does not have the ability to create these things. And thinking about the connections between these things also seemed like *en*.

The reason we decided to incorporate a guesthouse in part of the building was that our grandmother lives there alone now and increasing the opportunities for friends and family to visit her would ensure that she would be looked after a little bit more. The reason we opted for separate wings was that it allowed us to control the distance between the guesthouse and our grandmother's house, and also that the inner courtyard, which was created after the structure was dismantled, would be a place for people to gather. This type of structure also seems to be connected to *en*.

Some people said moving the roof was overdoing things. But the fact was that that helped cut costs and moving it also became a festive occasion. In this way, the roof, fixed in one place for many years, conveyed a sense of lively movement. And by creating a staged connection between the acts of destruction and creation, things were assembled in the midst of movement and flow.

The various things in *Guest House in Takaoka* might have ended up there by accident. But the fact that they had been there over a certain period of time gave them a unique quality. *En* is a form that can be used to makes sense of randomness. Using the word *en* in regard to things like chance encounters helps us understand our environment and the events that happen in our lives. Though the environment we live in is filled with random occurrences, we can use it to create a feeling of certainty in these encounters. We see the role of architecture as manifesting and supporting the certainty of *en*.

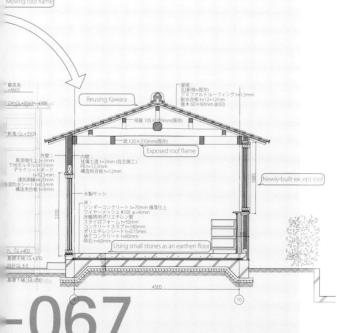

環境への視点の転換から、新たな空間と関係性を生み出す

Creating a New Space and Relationship by Altering a View of the Environment

今村水紀＋篠原勲／miCo.
Mizuki Imamura＋Isao Shinohara／miCo.

駒沢公園の家
House at Komazawa Park
TOKYO | 2011

東京の木造密集地域における住宅の改修。高度経済成長期の都心では、敷地は細分化され、たくさんの住宅がひしめくように建てられた。その多くは、日本の木造在来軸組構法でつくられている。在来軸組構法は、尺貫法というモデュールを用いたシンプルなルールの構造であり、文化というかたちで広く受け継がれている。この住宅は、柱梁を継いだり抜いたりできる木造軸組の可変性を生かして、既存の建物をふたつの建物に分け、新築を含めた小さな3つの建物群へと再構成している。この建物単位の変更は、敷地境界を越えて、周囲の木造密集地の風景更新の可能性までも示唆しているように見える。

3つの建物同士の隙間は、外の光や地面を引き込み、部屋同士を緩やかに隔てると同時に繋げており、内と外、内と内の相互浸透が起こっている。既存の木軸と新規の構造が違和感なく同時にあり、古いものと新しいものが渾然一体となった明るくみずみずしい空間が生まれている。

This renovation project was undertaken in a section of Tokyo with a high concentration of wooden buildings. During the high-economic growth period, lots in the city center were segmented and houses were packed together. Many were built using conventional Japanese, post-and-beam construction. This method, based on simple rules rooted in the traditional Japanese measuring system, was widely perpetuated as a form of culture.

This work made the most of the variable nature of this construction method, which allows for the addition and subtraction of posts and beams, to divide the existing structure into two buildings and restructure the house into a group of three small buildings, including a new one. This modification of the architectural unit extends beyond the confines of the lot, suggesting various possibilities for renovating the landscape of the surrounding, densely populated area.

1｜敷地は、旗竿状敷地となっており、細分化され、庭や駐車場をもたない住宅がぎっしりと並ぶ環境にある。住宅地を骨格レベルで捉えると、表層のデザインの違いだけではなく、木造密集地の、建物の大きさや形を変えることで、風景の更新ができるのではないかと考えた。
2｜改修前の築約30年の木造住宅。南に小さな庭をもつなど、周りの住宅に比べて少し余白があるため、増築を含めた改築が計画された。
3｜施工中の様子。既存住宅をふたつに分け、庭にとても小さな小屋を新築し、3つの建物が現れた。既存建物の木の軸組を最大限利用する計画のため、開口部の位置は、既存を踏襲したものとなっている。
4｜引き渡し後の東側外観。3つの建物の間は背の高いガラスで繋いでいる。建物のスケールを小さくしたことで、家具や洗濯物といった日常のもの、物置や植物が、存在感をもって現れてきた。隣の畑も含め、敷地境界を越えて、環境が緩やかに繋がっているように感じられる。

1｜The flagpole lot is segmented, has neither a garden nor a parking space, and is an area that is closely packed with houses. By viewing the residential area as a basic framework, we thought by not only altering the design superficially but also changing the size and shape of the house in this densely concentrated area of wooden buildings, we would be able to renew the landscape.
2｜The approximately 30-year-old wooden building before the renovation. As it had a little more open space than the surrounding houses (there was a small garden on the south side, etc.), we planned a renovation that included an extension.
3｜The house under construction. By dividing the house into two, and building a new hut in the garden, we ended up with three buildings. As the plan attempted to maximize the wooden framework of the existing house, the position of the openings remained the same.
4｜Exterior of the east side after the project was completed. The three buildings are connected by tall pieces of glass. By minimizing the scale of the buildings, everyday objects like furniture and laundry as well as storage spaces and plants emerged as presences. Extending beyond the boundaries of the lot to include things like the field next door, the environment seemed to be loosely connected.

House at Komazawa Park　Mizuki Imamura＋Isao Shinohara　miCo.

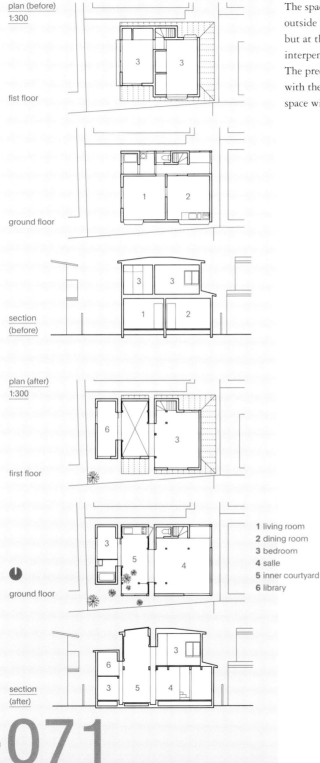

plan (before) 1:300

fist floor

ground floor

section (before)

plan (after) 1:300

first floor

1 living room
2 dining room
3 bedroom
4 salle
5 inner courtyard
6 library

ground floor

section (after)

The spaces between the three buildings draw in outside light and ground, and gently separate but at the same time link the rooms, lading to interpenetration between the interior and exterior. The preexisting wooden axis comfortably coexists with the new building, creating a bright and lustrous space with a perfect harmony of old and new.

インタビュー｜06｜今村水紀＋篠原勲／miCo.

Q｜「en（縁）」というテーマについてどのように考えて参加されましたか？

「縁」というのは、何かと何かの間（あいだ）に起こる関係性のかたちである、という気がしています。「間（ま）」が中心にある空っぽの空間をイメージさせるのに対して、縁は、境界に発生している、細長い形のようなものが思い浮かびます。また、間（ま）は、広場のように最初から計画が可能なもので、縁は複数のものを計画した時にその境界に生まれる、2次的な副産物のようにも感じました。そしてその性質上、縁は完結しない、コントロールできない領域を含んでいるのではないかと思います。

「駒沢公園の家」では、既存の建物という、コントロールできない領域を含む環境を受け入れ、少しでも状況が良くなるような更新の仕方を考えました。計画当初は、建築要素のすべてを設計対象とすることができないリノベーションに、ストレスを感じていましたが、スタディを進めるにつれ、可能性を感じられるようになりました。そこには発想の転換がありました。計画住戸を含めた周辺を、住宅という個の集合ではなく、木造軸組の密集している環境と捉えたのです。

木造は、スクラップ・アンド・ビルドが容易な構造というイメージがありますが、一方で、切ったり継いだりできる更新が容易なサステナブルな構造とも言えます。また、在来軸組構法は、文化というかたちで受け継がれてきた、尺貫法という910mmのモジュールに則ったシンプルな構造でもあります。軸組が密集している様を想像した時に、住宅密集地という厳しい状況が、建築の単位を変えることでさまざまな環境が生まれる可能性や希望に満ちた状況に見えてきました。たとえば、隣接

section 1:100

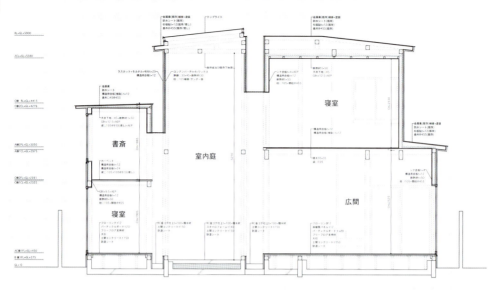

House at Komazawa Park　Mizuki Imamura＋Isao Shinohara　miCo.

1｜室内庭には、本やCD、食器や花瓶を置き、洗濯物も干している。室内でも明るい庭のような空間には、雑多な環境を受け入れる質がある。
2｜改修プロセスを示す木造軸組模型。1階の面積を増やすことが望まれた。しかし、建物を大きくすると、周りの環境に影響を与える。そこで、3つの小さな小屋を建てることを考えた。b：まず、元の建物を切断し、ふたつの小屋に分けた。c：敷地南にあった暗い庭を、真ん中の小屋に移動し、いずれ周囲を建物で囲まれる旗竿状敷地の中央を明るくすることを考えた。d：もともと庭だった場所に新しい小屋を建てた。周辺への圧迫感もなくなり、建物の単位が小さくなったことで、外部と親密になり、光や風を採り入れやすくなった。
3｜ひとつながりの室内に屋外が入り込んでいるため、室内にいながら都市の路地を通るような瞬間が訪れる。
4｜室内庭は、トップライトを含め、開口部を多く設けている。光に満ちた空間が、建築の真ん中に現れ出ている。
5｜敷地中央の吹き抜けが、他の棟の、空間の質の違う小さな部屋同士を緩やかに繋いでいる。
6｜内部と内部、内部と外部の相互浸透が起こり、古い材と新しい材が同時に存在する環境。

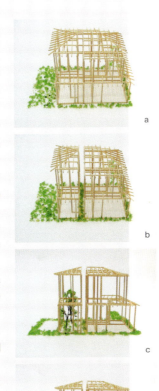

a

b

c

d

2

1｜The inside garden contains things like books, CDs, dishes, and vases, and the laundry can also be hung there. Even inside, the bright garden-like space seems to incorporate various environments.
2｜A wooden framework model illustrating the renovation process. The client had hoped to increase the area on the first floor. But if the size of the building was increased, it would affect the surrounding environment. That led us to the idea of making three huts. b: We started by cutting the existing building into two huts. c: Then we moved the dark garden on the south side to the hut in the center with the idea of brightening up the center of the flagpole lot that was surrounded by houses. d: Then we built a new hut where the original garden had been. This alleviated the oppressive feeling caused by the surroundings, and by making each building unit smaller, it was easier to create a sense of intimacy with the outside and to allow more light and wind inside.

するふたつの軸組も、大きなひとつの建築に更新することもできると想像したのです。

尺貫法のモジュールや木造密集地という環境を受け入れることによって、建物同士の隙間の扱い方が変わり、建築の単位の捉え方が変わりました。大きなワンルームの内部空間の間に、隙間である外部が引き込まれていたり、古い材と新しい材が同時に存在することで生まれる環境は、既存建物があるからこそ可能になりました。この多様な状況を多様なままに扱い、さまざまな関係性が生み出されている環境を成立させている建築が、縁の建築なのではないかと考えました。

このリノベーションを手がけたことによって、多様な状況を一度受け入れ、関係性について考えること、つまり縁について考えることに気づいたように思います。それによって、新築も含めた建築の設計が、これから少し変わるのではないかという気がしています。

Interview｜06｜
Mizuki Imamura + Isao Shinohara／miCo.

Q｜How did you approach the theme of *en* in this exhibition?

We have the sense that *en* is a form of connection that arises between two things. Unlike *ma*, which recalls an empty space in the center of something, *en* suggests a long thin shape that emerges along a border. *Ma* is also something that can be pre-planned, such as a square, but *en* is something secondary, a byproduct that arises from a boundary when plans are made for a group of things. And in terms of its qualities, *en* seems to include areas that cannot be completed or controlled.

In this house, we accepted the environment, which included the uncontrollable area of the existing building, and we considered how we might improve the situation even a little bit. At the outset, the idea of a renovation project, which does not allow you to design every architectural element, was stressful, but as we moved forward

House at Komazawa Park Mizuki Imamura + Isao Shinohara miCo.

3 | When the outside entered the connected interior, it suddenly seemed as if you were passing through an urban alley while still inside.
4 | Many openings, including a top light, were created for the inner garden. A light-filled space emerged in the center of the building.
5 | The atrium in the center of the lot loosely connects the small rooms, each with a different spatial quality, in all of the wings.
6 | A state of interpenetration arose between the inside spaces, and the inside and outside, creating an environment in which old and new materials existed side-by-side.

with our studies, we started to sense various potentials. That led to a change in our thinking. Instead of seeing the house as an individual assemblage that included the surrounding area, we began to look at it as a dense environment of wooden frameworks.

Though wooden buildings are often seen as simple scrap-and-build structures, a renewal project, which can either break or maintain a connection, can also be seen as a simple sustainable structure. In addition, the conventional post-and-beam building method manifests simple structures, which rely on the 910 mm module (rooted in the traditional Japanese measuring system) and have been carried on as a form of culture. When we imagined a mass of frameworks, we began to see a situation that was filled with the potential and hope for a variety of emerging environments based on modifying the architectural unit. For example, you might re-envision two adjacent frameworks by renovating them into a single large building.

By accepting the traditional measuring module and the dense area of wooden buildings, our understanding of the gaps between the buildings changed, and our way of looking at architectural units also changed. By doing something like drawing an outside gap into the interior of a large one-room space, the resulting environment, in which old and new materials exist side-by-side, becomes possible for the very reason that there is a preexisting building. By dealing with such diverse conditions in diverse ways, we came to believe that architecture which creates an environment with a variety of connections is an architecture of *en*.

In this renovation project, we accepted a wide range of conditions all at once and began to thinking about the nature of connection; in other words, we came to realize that we were considering *en*. As a result, we have the sense that our future designs, including those for new buildings, will be different.

レビ設計室
Levi Architecture

15Aの家

15A House

TOKYO | 2016

人間と環境の
関係を深く問い直し、
あらたな繋がりを
再生する

Regenerating
Connections
by Thoroughly Reexamining
the Relationship
between Human Beings
and the Environment

この住宅は東京都心に近い住宅密集地で施工中の建築家の自邸である。2011年の震災と原発事故を契機に、建築家は、この死と隣り合わせの問題と共存するためには、今までの仕事と生活を深く反省し、己の身体感覚を手仕事のレベルから鍛え直す必要があると考えた。

地震に強いこと、建築家自身によって施工可能なこと、家族4人が15アンペア（100V・15A）の制約の中で不自由なく暮らせること——この3つを条件として設計が進められた。改修の際に骨組みに近い状態にまで還元された住宅空間の建築性を担保したまま技術（art and technology）によって人が住み得る環境にしようとするのだけれども、快適な環境には決して達し得ないこの住みにくさに対し、そこに住まう人間の主体的な努力によって乗り越えようとする崇高さ（conviviality）を獲得するために、住宅の機能を最小限に抑えつつ、生存に必要な光・熱・風といった環境を取り込む操作が綿密な解析のもと行われた。

This house, currently under construction in a densely populated part of central Tokyo, is the architect Jun Nakagawa's private residence. Following the earthquake and nuclear power plant accident that occurred in eastern Japan in 2011, Nakagawa began to carefully reexamine his work and life in order to deal with the issue of living side-by-side with death. He ultimately decided it was necessary to return to a manual approach to retrain his physical sensibilities.

The design for this house is based on three conditions: a strong resistance to earthquakes, a construction method that can be implemented by the architect himself, and the ability for a family of four to live comfortably on a maximum of 15 amps (100V・1500W) of electric current. By using art and technology to imbue a residential space, which has been to reduced to a virtual framework in the renovation process, with an architectural quality, the architects tried to create an environment for people to live. At the same time, in order to achieve

15A House Levi Architecture

078-

a conviviality that transcends these decidedly inconvenient living conditions in a comfortable environment through the active efforts of the residents, they created a design in which the functions of the house were kept to a bare minimum and operations involving environmental factors such as light, heat, and wind, which are necessary for survival, were subjected to an in-depth analysis.

インタビュー｜07｜レビ設計室

Q｜「en（縁）」というテーマについてどのように考えて参加されましたか？

「縁」という言葉には、前向きに事物が連鎖していく、発見的で、驚きに満ちた世界のイメージがありますが、「15Aの家」は、前向きな「縁」とは程遠い位置にあるもの、つまり事物の連鎖を止めること、縁を断ち切るところからスタートしなければ何も始まらないという「縁」の自生の問題を扱っています。

2011年5月に写真家の山岸剛さんのスタジオで東北の写真を見せてもらう機会がありました。「田老」と名付けられた被写体は津波の被害を受けた倉庫で、朱色の錆止めがあらわになった鉄骨の躯体と、そこに絡まる瓦礫の構図にひどく無意識を揺さぶられたことを今でも覚えています。「田老」の写真から、建築とは別次元に存在する自然の姿を、建築＝廃墟を通して感じたわけですが、そこには圧倒的な脅威の裏側に存在する自然の美しさも同時に映し出されており、建築が本来もっている姿と、今までそれを描くことができなかった私の感性の鈍さを同時に突きつけられ、しばらく建築を設計することができなくなりました。その反動でしょうか、「15Aの家」の解体時にはつねに「田老」を意識することになりました。

千年に一度の津波は、福島第一原発にも大きなダメージを与えました。そこから排出された放射性物質は人類の歴史よりも遙かに永い、建築の射程では到底捉えきれない時間を伴って風土を分断しました。高度成長期に入りエネルギー消費量が増え、これに呼応するかたちで原発が増設されたわけですが、無自覚なエネルギーの使用と引

1｜「2011年5月1日 岩手県宮古市田老青砂利」。山岸剛による写真。彼はこの写真について「建築はかつてないほど健康に見えた」と述べており、「15Aの家」を解体する時にはつねに「田老」の光を意識した。

2｜完成予想パース。屋根のバラ板の隙間から降り注ぐ光の驟雨（しゅうう）によって気づく都市の自然もある。既存の古い構造体に挿入した直交長押は、2層吹き抜けの空間すべてを使い、風と光をコントロールする。

3｜コンセプト模型。模型に用いた鉄骨の表現は解体の経験から必然的に生まれたものである。鉄は錆びることでゆっくり風化し、土に還る。金槌で叩きヤスリで削ると表情を変え、熱を加えるとゆがむ。既存部分の個人的な歴史とリテラルな経年変化を、素人の荒々しい溶接で表現した。

1 | Blue gravel in Taro, Miyako, Iwate Prefecture, May 1, 2011. The photograph was taken by Takeshi Yamagishi, who commented, "Architecture never looked so healthy." In dismantling *15A House*, I was constantly aware of the light in Taro.

2 | Visualized perspective view of completed work. The shower of light that pours down through the gaps in the roof board sheeting prompts an awareness of urban nature. The horizontal tie beams from the old structure were used in the second-floor atrium to control the wind and light.

3 | Photo of concept model. The expression of the model's steel frame naturally grew out of the experience of dismantling the building. The steel slowly weathers as it rusts and returns to the earth. The expression was modified by striking it with a hammer and shaving it with a file, and distorting its shape with heat. The changing personal history of the existing parts and the literal passage of time are expressed through the rough amateur welding.

plan 1:300

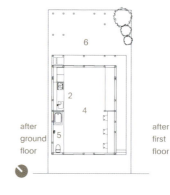
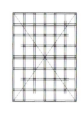

before ground floor | before first floor | after ground floor | after first floor

1 entrance
2 kitchen
3 Japanese-style room
4 room
5 bathroom
6 garden

1

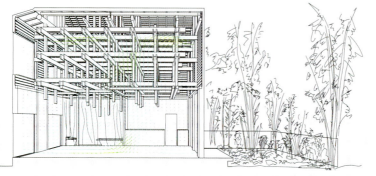

2

1｜改修前平面図(左)と改修後平面図(右)。築50年(増築部35年)の木造2階建て住宅を改修する。平屋部分および2階の床部分を撤去減築し、地震力を軽減させるとともに、吹き抜け空間を利用して光と風を内部に採り込む。平面計画は未定で、つくりながら考えていく。

2｜断面パース。外皮性能を上げながらも、光を最大限採り入れる。熱は吹き抜けを利用して、貫流熱と人体からの発熱を足し合わせた熱を排出する風環境とした。

3｜構造概略図。築50年と35年の2階既存フレームに直交長押を挿入した。

4｜直交長押構法概略図。柱芯上に打たれたファスナーと、相互に2方向に直交するツーバイ材同士の接触点とで、テコのように曲げモーメントに対して抵抗する仕組みとなっている。直交長押構法の利点は、施工の簡易さであり、小屋組みや独立柱の補強が非常に容易な点にある。

5｜直交長押構法接合部曲げ実験。

1｜Pre-renovation floor plan (left); post-renovation floor plan (right). The project involved renovating a two-story, 50-year-old wooden house (with a 35-year-old extension). Removing and reducing the one-story section and the floor on the second level lessened the risk of earthquakes, and allowed light and outside wind into the space via the atrium. The floor plan was undecided, taking shape as the project evolved.

2｜Sectional perspective. While improving the function of the outer skin, this design maximized the amount of light in the house. Due to the atrium, the wind environment eliminated both the heat generated by transmission and people's bodies.

3｜Schematic drawing of the structure. Horizontal tie beams were incorporated into the existing 50- and 35-year-old existing framework on the second floor.

4｜Tie-beam construction diagram. Driving fasteners into the top of the core column and forming an intersection between two-by-fours that crossed at right angles created a mechanism that counteracted a lever-like bending moment. The advantages of the horizontal tie beam construction were the simplicity of the construction and the ease with which the roof truss and free-standing columns could be reinforced.

5｜Photo of an experiment in which the joints were bent in a orthogonal tie-beam construction.

15A House Levi Architecture

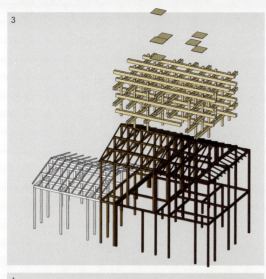

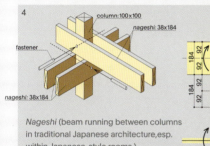

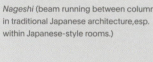

Nageshi (beam running between columns in traditional Japanese architecture, esp. within Japanese-style rooms.)

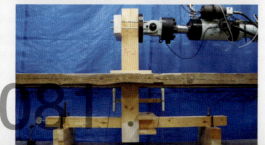

き換えに、私たちは大切なものを失いました。この問題に対峙するためには、時代の制約に縛られた先端技術とは異なる思想を内包した技術で応えなければなりません。「15Aの家」は15Aという制約の中で生活を営む住宅です。制約の概念は、イヴァン・イリイチの『エネルギーと公正』にあるエネルギー危機を乗り越えるための条件を参照しており、実現するのは極めて難しいけれども「エネルギーに制約をもたなければならない(ceiling on energy)」という思想を踏襲しています。

「田老」が示唆した建築が本来もっている姿と、15Aの制約の統合は非常な困難を伴います。建築というフレームでこの問題に対峙する限り、技術で乗り越えなければなりません。バークやカントは崇高の美学という概念を提示していますが、これは理性的な判断によって困難を克服することで得られる概念でした。決して十分ではないけれども、建築の技術と、主体的な行動を通じて環境を自らのものにできるかどうか、つまり人間と環境との関係を深く問い直した上で、新たな「縁」を再生することが「15Aの家」の目的なのです。

Interview | 07 | Levi Architecture

Q | How did you approach the theme of *en* in this exhibition?

Though the word *en* calls up images of a world in which a chain of things are linked in a positive way, and one that is heuristic and filled with surprise, *15 A House* is far removed from this sort of situation. Instead, it deals with the inherent problem of *en* as something that can only start after the chain has been interrupted and the *en* severed.

In May 2011, I had an opportunity to visit Takeshi Yamagishi's studio to see his photographs of the Tohoku region taken after the earthquake earlier that year. I still remember how I was unconsciously shaken by the composition of the subject, called "Taro." The vermilion rust-proofing of the warehouse's steel framework was exposed, and the building was entwined with a heap of rubble. The photograph gave

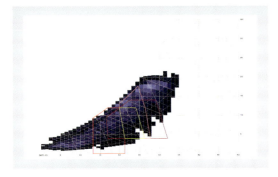
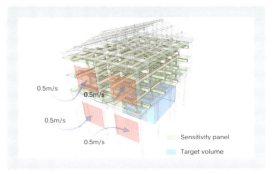

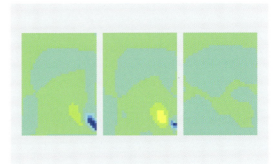
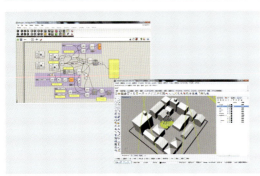
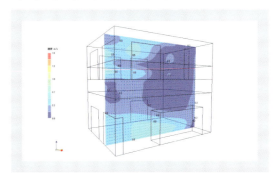
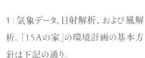

1 | 気象データ、日射解析、および風解析。「15Aの家」の環境計画の基本方針は下記の通り。
a) 外皮性能の向上（断熱改修計画）
b) 日射取得と通風の最適化（構造計画との融合）

解析の結果、設計目標は達成できるが、15Aの制約の中で暮らすためには、住まい手の主体的な意思と、建築を触覚的に受容するプロセスが必要である。
2 | 2012年夏の消費エネルギー。15Aの制約を設けることは空調の使用に制約が生じることが分かった。このため空調機によって快適性を担保するのではなく、建築の形態で温熱環境を担保できないか考えた。
3 | 厳しい条件下では空調機を使うこともあり得るので、全体の使用量が15Aを超えないようにサイリスタ位相制御装置をコンセントに組み込むと同時に、15Aの制約を無理なく受け入れるため、最大容量に近付くと照明等によって切迫した状況を伝えるシステムも合わせて開発した。
4 | 制御システムの回路図。

1 | Meteorological data, and a breakdown of sunlight and wind. The basic policy for the environmental plan in *15A House* was as follows:
a) Improve the function of the outer skin (insulation retrofitting plan)
b) Optimize intake of sunlight and ventilation (fusion with the

15A House　Levi Architecture

082-

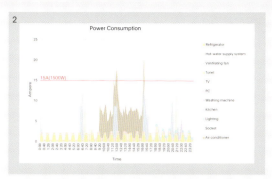

2

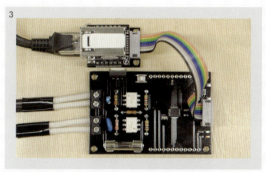

3

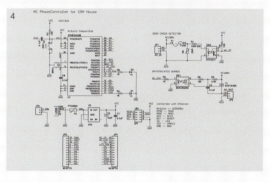

4

me the sense that architecture conveyed the appearance of nature, which dwells in a different dimension, through the rubble. While simultaneously depicting the beauty of nature, backed with an ominous threat, architecture's intrinsic form collided with my dull sensibilities, which had prevented me from depicting this aspect in the past, and left me unable to design anything. Then as a kind of reaction, as I was dismantling *15 A House*, I remained constantly aware of Taro.

The once-in-a-millennium tsunami greatly damaged the Fukushima Daiichi Nuclear Power Station. The radioactive material emitted from the plant will affect the climate for a temporal period that cannot be grasped in architectural terms, forever altering human history. Japan's period of high economic growth saw an increase in energy consumption and nuclear power plants were increased to this need, but in unconsciously using energy in this way, we lost something important. To deal with this problem, we must respond with technology based on a different philosophy than state-of-the-art technology that was limited by the era. *15 A House* forces the resident to live according to 15 A (1500 W) restrictions. This refers to the conditions for overcoming an energy crisis as explained in Ivan Illich's *Energy and Equity*. Though very difficult to realize, the idea is to place a "ceiling on energy."

It was extremely difficult to unify the original form of the building suggested by Taro with the 15 A restrictions. As long as we try to confront these problems within an architectural framework, technology will be necessary. Burke and Kant posited an aesthetics based on the sublime, but this was a concept based on conquering hardships through intellectual judgment. That is by no means sufficient. The aim of *15 A House* is trigger new *en* by closely reexamining the potential for creating an environment with architectural techniques and autonomous actions – in other words, making a connection between human beings and the environment.

structural plan)
As a result of the analysis, the design objectives were achieved, but in order to live within the restrictions of the 15 A law, it was necessary for the resident to arrive at an independent idea and accept the building on a tactile level.
2 | Energy consumption in the summer of 2012. The 15 A limitations clearly limited the use of air conditioning. Thus, instead of maintaining the comfort level with an air conditioner, it seemed possible to sustain a thermal environment with the building's form.
3 | Because using the air conditioner was an option in harsh conditions, the sockets were equipped with thyristor phase control devices to ensure that total energy use would not exceed 15 A limitations. At the same time, to accept the limitations in a reasonable manner, a system was developed to indicate when the lights were on the verge of reaching maximum capacity.
4 | Circuit board for the control system.

増田信吾+大坪克亘
Shingo Masuda+Katsuhisa Otsubo Architects

躯体の窓
Boundary Window

CHIBA | 2014

084

前提条件=関係性を
デザインすることにより、
場所を組み立て直す

**Reassembling a Place
by Designing Preexisting Conditions
or Relationships**

建物の縮小傾向や建築部材の工業化に伴って、建築空間に対する窓や壁といったエレメントの重要性とその影響力は建築の内外を問わず強まっている。この「躯体の窓」は、鉄筋コンクリートの既存の2階建ての建物より大きく3層分にまで拡大された窓で、室内と庭の両方がもっている前提条件を変えている。この拡大された窓により、サッシ、ガラス戸、カーテンは建物の開口部に納めず、それぞれを庭側へとずらすことで拡大し、エレメントに内在する関係性を建築の全体へと変換している。全面ガラスは太陽光を反射し、庭へと十分な光をもたらすため、敷地の入隅まで光が届き、以前は暗かった冬期にも明るい庭になった。2階開口部の手摺がガラス戸のレールとしても機能し、窓を開けた時、開口部には必要なもの以外は残らない。窓の可能性が引き出され、窓という境界が空間を揺るがし、身体と環境に対する拡張された感覚を生み出している。

Due to the tendency to reduce the size of buildings and the industrialization of building components, the importance and influence of elements such as windows and walls in architectural spaces has grown, both in regard to the interior and exterior. In *Boundary Window*, the architect used an enlarged window to greatly expand the original two-story, reinforced-concrete building, changing the preconditions of the interior and the garden. The window enabled the architect to move the sash, glass door, and curtain toward the garden without obstructing any of the building's openings, and shift the innate relationship between the elements to the building as a whole. The all-glass surface reflects sunlight, providing the garden with an adequate amount of light, and conveying it to the internal corners of the lot, so that the garden, which in the past was dark during the winter, is now bright. The handrail on the second floor opening also functions as the rail for the glass door. When it is opened, nothing remains except the handrail. By drawing out the potential of the window, its function as a boundary alters the space, giving rise to an expanded perception of the body and environment.

8枚のカーテン、窓枠、そして上下合わせて16枚のガラス戸で構成されている。1枚のガラス戸は幅がおおよそ1.7m、高さ4mであり、人が軽やかに動かせるようガラスの厚みとそれを支えるスチール量のバランスが考えられている。戸は、風圧を考慮して、ガラスが割れることなく75mm程度歪むことを許容する設計となっている。風速34m/sでおおよそ35mm歪む計算である。どちらかというと堅固な建物の一部というよりはファサードを覆う膜として捉えられる。

The window consists of eight curtains, window frames, and a total of 16 glass doors on two levels. Each door has a width of about 1.7 meters and a height of four meters. The design strikes a balance between glass that is thin enough for someone to open and enough steel to support the glass. In light of the wind pressure, the glass was produced to withstand about 75 mm warpage. The warpage was calculated at about 35 mm in winds of 34 meters per second. Rather than being part of a solid building, it is like a membrane covering the facade.

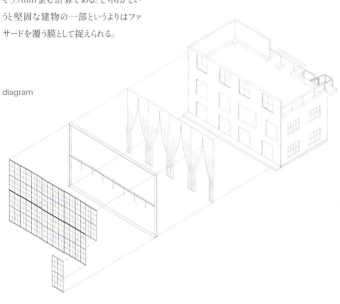

diagram

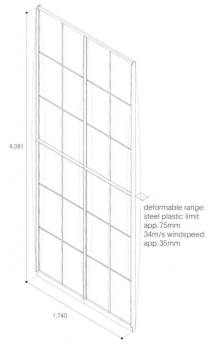

deformable range:
steel plastic limit
app. 75mm
34m/s windspeed:
app. 35mm

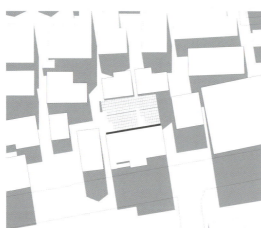

site plan 1:800

before

086-

Boundary Window　Shingo Masuda + Katsuhisa Otsubo Architects

plan 1:300

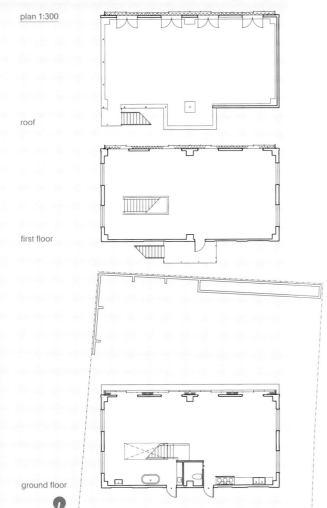

roof

first floor

ground floor

インタビュー｜08｜増田信吾＋大坪克亘

Q｜「en（縁）」というテーマについてどのように考えて参加されましたか？

僕たちが物心ついた時には新幹線が走っていて、ディズニーランドもあり、東京はすでに今と変わらない大都市で、レジャーや生活に必要とされるものはそろっていて、僕らは不自由を感じた記憶がありません。そういう意味で、建築も何かを満たすために創造するという直接的なアプローチよりも、何か他のモノと関係するモノとして捉えることに可能性を感じています。

そもそも関係性は、たとえ予備知識を蓄えても、たとえ計画的に行っても、結局はとても奇跡的な偶然の巡り合わせで、何かを介して巻き起こるものであるため、「縁」なのではないかと思います。もし関係性によって場所を組み立てることができたら、場所自体だけでなく、建物、人など、さまざまな事柄が窮屈に分けられることなく、それぞれがもっと対等で自由に存在できるのではないかと思っています。場所性がどうしたら計画できるのか、空間や建物自体をつくるのではなく、それらに影響を与え、まったく違う状況を創造できるのか。「躯体の窓」は一見ただ窓を大きく設計しているように見えるのですが、場所がもつ前提的な条件を、窓を介して設計しようとしました。

初めて敷地を訪れたのは秋でした。庭は建物の南側にあるにもかかわらず、向かい側の建物の影によってとても暗かった。でもクライアントにはその庭を植物でいっぱいにしたいという希望がありました。そして既存建物の開口部のアルミサッシを取り替えて、まったく新しい庭と室内の関係を求めていました。僕たちは内装や庭がもってしまっている前提を揺るがすような前提条件の設計の必要を感じていたので、そこを任せてもらいました。

設計した窓は建物よりもおおよそ1層分高く、薄いガラスを使用することで庭側への太陽光の反射を最大化し暗い冬の庭を照らします。夏でも陽が当たらないような隅にも光が届くようになり、塀沿いに花壇を設けることができるようになりまし

ガラス面が日差しを反射し、暗い庭を照らす。よって、この庭は植物や人の影が通常の逆に伸びていくため、とても人工的な環境である。冬には、反射によって夏でも光が届かない入隅にまで光が届いて日射状況が良くなるため、自由な植栽計画が可能になっている。周りは建物で囲まれているため、周囲に対しても明るいコートヤードになっている。

The glass surface reflects sunlight, illuminating the dark garden. Since this elongates the shadows of plants and people, it is a very artificial environment. In winter, the reflection improves the lighting conditions so that sunlight extends into the corners, where even in the summer it does not usually reach, making it possible to plant things freely. As the site is surrounded by other buildings, this area functions as a bright courtyard.

Boundary Window Shingo Masuda + Katsuhisa Otsubo Architects

088-

内部にとって自然なスケールと外部にとって自然なスケールは異なるはず、と考えた。内側からは小割りにされた普通の窓として存在し、外へはヒューマンスケールを超えた存在となることで、庭や敷地全体をおおらかにしている。

The natural scale inside seemed to differ from the natural scale outside. By making a regular, thinly divided window inside, and creating an entity that transcended human scale outside, the design imbued the garden and the overall area with a relaxed atmosphere.

た。そして全体が窓になることで、以前は開けた窓の数によって外との繋がり具合が決まっていたのですが、今ではそれがどの程度の割合で窓を開放したかによって場所全体の繋がり具合が決まるようになっています。ガラス戸は上下2段にすることでちょうど2階の手摺としても機能するようになっているので、開けた時、開口部にはサッシなどの余計なものが残らず、とても開放的な場所になります。

そこに人が介入した時、いろいろな事柄が結び付き関係性によって場所が成り立っていく、それはとても自然だと僕らは感じています。場所がもつ関係性を計画することは、まさに「モノの縁」というテーマに即したことなのではないか、と思っています。

Interview | 08 | Shingo Masuda ＋ Katsuhisa Otsubo Architects

Q | How did you approach the theme of *en* in this exhibition?

As long as we can remember, the Shinkansen has been running, Disneyland was there, and Tokyo was a huge metropolis. Everything you need for leisure and living is available and as far as we can recall we've never experienced any kind of inconvenience. In that sense, rather than using a direct approach in which you try to make architecture that satisfies a certain purpose, you can conceive of it as something related to other things.

Whether it's based on an accumulation of preliminary knowledge, or a plan, relationships are ultimately miraculous accidents that cause things to happen – I think of this as *en*. If you can assemble a place based on relationships, it is not merely a place. It is impossible to divide up the various factors, such as buildings and people, there; they exist independently as equals. How do you go about planning the character of a place? It has nothing to do with making the space and building themselves; it's about whether you can create a set of completely different

カーテン、カーテンレール、サッシ、戸、手摺、といった建物を閉じていくための要素は建物の少し外側で全体に対して設置しているため、窓を閉めた時でも室内は開放的で、庭との接続を感じることができる場所になっている。シングルガラスが生む熱は建物に到達する前に煙突効果によって屋上の方へ流れるようになっている。

As elements such as curtains, curtain rails, sashes, doors, and handrails to close up the building were all installed slightly outside of the whole, even when the windows are closed, the inside is an open place that seems connected to the garden. The heat that is generated by a single sheet of glass flows up to the roof due to a chimney effect before reaching the rest of the building.

Boundary Window   Shingo Masuda + Katsuhisa Otsubo Architects

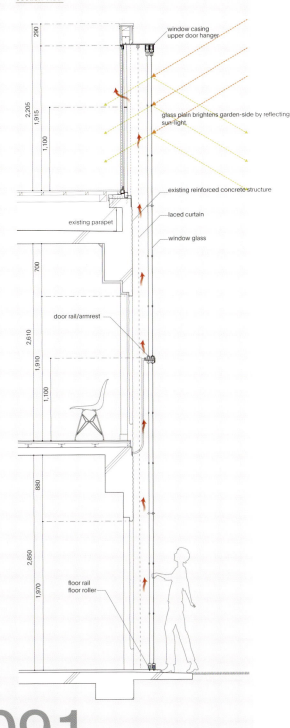

section 1:50

circumstances in which these things influence each other. Although *Boundary Window* initially appears to have been designed as a large window, it was actually an attempt to design the preconditions contained in the place by means of the window.

It was fall when I first visited the site. Despite the fact that the garden was on the south side, the shadow of the opposing building made it very dark. The clients, however, hoped to fill the garden with plants. And they also wanted to replace the aluminum sashes on the windows in the existing building and create a completely new relationship between the garden and the interior. Since we felt the need to design preconditions that altered the existing relationship between the interior and the garden, we were entrusted with that.

The window we designed was about a floor higher than the building, and by using thin sheets of glass, we were able to maximize the light reflected into the garden and illuminate the space, which was dark in winter. The light even reached corners where the sun had never shined in summer, making it possible to install flowerbeds along the wall. When you made something entirely of glass in the past, the relationship with the outside depended on the number of windows that were open. Prior to the renovation, the relationship with the outside depended on the number of windows that were open. And by making two levels of glass doors, they also function as handrails for the second floor. When they are open, there are no superfluous parts, such as sashes, around the openings, creating an extremely open place.

When people enter the space, a variety of elements are linked and the relationships that arise as a result create a place with very natural conditions. To us, it seems that planning the relationships in a place fits in perfectly with the theme of the *en* of things.

en: art of nexus

Padiglione Giappone Biennale Architettura 2016

-091

スクラップ・アンド・ビルドが都市成長のロールモデルとして機能しなくなっている場所において、建物のエレメントに注目しながら、どのような材料をどこから調達するかといった、モノのネットワークを設計対象とし、新築、改修、あるいは解体といったカテゴライズを横断した「マテリアルの流動」の中に建築を位置付けようとする一連の試みである。「渥美の床」では天井の野縁をカットして床に敷き詰め、「頭陀寺の壁」では現場の解体で生じた廃材と廃棄予定の木製パレットをミックス。「富塚の天井」では農業用のネットを天井材に転用している。これらは、地方都市を拠点として、重点的に場所と結び付いたリサーチと実践を繰り返すことで、一つひとつのプロジェクトは小規模なものでありながらも、都市そのものと直接かかわり得るような、多発する出来事としての建築群である。

In a place where the "scrap-and-build" approach no longer functions as a model for urban growth, the architects conducted a series of experiments in an effort to locate architecture in a flux of materials that transcends categories such as new construction, renovation, and dismantling. They set out to realize a design based on a network of things, which includes questions such as where a given material can be procured, while focusing on building elements.

In *The Floor of Atsumi*, the architects cut the ceiling joists and used them to cover the floor. In *The Wall of Zudaji*, they combined wood waste derived from a dismantling project on the site with wooden pallets that were also set to be thrown away. In *The Ceiling of Tomitsuka*, they converted agricultural nets into a ceiling material. Though each project is small, the architects, based in a regional city, create buildings as multiple occurrences with the potential to form a direct link with the city by repeatedly undertaking research and practices that are related to a given place.

大門の目地

The Joints of Daimon

HAMAMATSU | 2013

「渥美の床」では天井材を落として床へと変え、「大門の目地」では床材を組み上げて腰壁と天板へと変えた。「三展の格子」では、根太(ねだ)が梁に、床が柱に、梁が床に、それぞれ部材の断面寸法は残ったまま、より細かな架構へと組み替えられている。建材としての木は、伝統的な知恵の結晶であり、合理的な建設のために規格化と体系化とが成されている。それらを都市から現地調達し、再構成することで、既存の文脈と新しい空間との間に、即物的な関係を築いている。

特定の場所に積極的にかかわり、リバース・エンジニアリングのように空間をリサーチすることで、材料の質感や、性質、構法との関連性などが有機的に浮かび上がる。何かを壊すということは、直接的に何かをつくることへと繋がり得る。それは、いま現在この瞬間の空間と、歴史的とも言える長い時間との対話である。

In The Floor of Atsumi, we transformed the ceiling material into a floor, and in *The Joints of Daimon*, we assembled the floor material and changed it into retaining walls and a table top. In *The Grid of Santen*, the floor joists became beams, the floor became columns, and the beams became the floor. Retaining the sectional dimensions of each part, we rearranged them into a minute framework. As a material, the floor is a crystallization of traditional knowledge that has been standardized and systematized into a rational construction method. By procuring these materials locally and reconstructing them, it is possible to create a practical relationship between the existing context and a new space. By proactively engaging with a given place, and conducting reverse research akin to reverse engineering, an organic relationship arises between the texture of the materials, the characteristics of the place, and the construction method. Destroying something is directly connected to creating something. It is a dialogue between the space at this moment and a long of history.

三展の格子

The Grid of Santen

HAMAMATSU | 2011

インタビュー | 09 | 403architecture [dajiba]

Q 「en (縁)」というテーマについてどのように考えて参加されましたか?

われわれは、静岡県浜松市を拠点として活動しており、これまで手がけたプロジェクトの過半数が、事務所から直径1km以内に集中しているなど、特定の地域に密接にかかわって設計活動を展開することを模索しています。普段から人や「モノ」の、かなり具体的で直接的な関係性の中で建築を考えているため、今回の「縁」というテーマは、われわれにとっては実に馴染みやすいものでした。

ただ、「縁」を「関係性」だと考えると、あらゆる物事は関係性の中で成り立っているので、何にでも当てはまってしまいます。今回は「モノの縁」、というカテゴリーに分類されているということもあったので、われわれのプロジェクトにおいて、どのように「モノ」が見出され、新しい文脈に位置付けられているのかを示そうと考えました。

そのために、単体のプロジェクトを解説するのではなく、複数のプロジェクトについて、それぞれどのような「モノ」の捉え方がされたのかを展示しています。具体的にはBefore / Process / Afterの3段階の写真を、10プロジェクトすべて並列にして見せています。たとえば、「渥美の床」では天井が剥ぎ取られ、露出した野縁材の写真、それを細かく裁断し、床に敷き詰めている写真、「床」として完成した写真、というようなものです。また、実際の過程を時間で区切っているだけではなく、「富塚の天井」のように、畑に設置されている防風ネットが並ぶ、「遠州のからっ風」が厳しい浜松らしい風景をBeforeの写真に用いるなど、参照元として見出した「モノ」についても扱っています。

また、これまでのプロジェクトを紹介するだけではなく、「モノ」の縁を展示するならば、展示会場に直接「モノ」を展示したいと考えました。その時、これまでのプロジェクトの端材やモックアップのようなものを持っていくのではなく、場所と密接にかかわった「モノ」の展開を見せるため、ヴェネチアの材料を用いて、現地で「実物」を制作することに

頭陀寺の壁

The Wall of Zudaji

HAMAMATSU | 2011

上：運送会社から廃棄予定のパレットを回収｜中：解体後にも集成材のように貼り合わせる｜下：採光のため、適度に隙間を開けながらつくられたファサード｜Before: Salvaging pallets, set to be scrapped, from a shipping company. During: After dismantling them, we glued them together to create something resembling laminated wood. After: The facade contains moderate gaps to allow natural light inside.

「頭陀寺の壁」では、役目を終えて廃棄処分される予定だったパレットを解体し、集成材として構造部材をつくり、小さな「新築」の倉庫を建設した。そこには「海老塚の段差」の壁や床の材料も一部組み込まれている。大引（おおびき）はあまりに見事な材料だったので移動させることは諦め、短手に切断したのちスタックし、階段として配置し直している。「浜松の展開図」は、壁紙、合板フローリング、レンガなどの建材を、剥がしたり砕いたものを用いている。仏教において、誕生と滅びが流転し続ける世界観を表す、曼荼羅の形式にそれを乗せた。

新築か改築か、あるいは解体かということは、マテリアルがある地点からある地点へと移動し、形を変えているという視点からは、同じことである。つくる対象や敷地の範囲内だけを設計の対象とするのではなく、どのようにマテリアルを流動させるかが問題だ。

In *The Wall of Zudaji*, we dismantled some pallets that had outlived their use and were scheduled to be discarded, and used them as structural elements in laminated wood boards, constructing a small newly-built storehouse. Some of the wood was also combined with the wall and floor materials in *The Difference of Ebitsuka*. The lumber girders were such a splendid material that we abandoned the idea of moving them out. After cutting and stacking them, we rearranged them to function as stairs. In *The Development of Hamamatsu*, we stripped away and crushed materials such as wallpaper, plywood flooring, and bricks. These were used to make a mandala, representing the Buddhist cosmology of continual transmigration of the soul.

From the perspective of transporting a material from one point to another and altering a form, the acts of newly constructing, renovating and dismantling something are the same. Instead of limiting your design to the scope of the subject or lot, the question is how you can make the material flow.

上：間仕切り壁、天井、床の半分を解体｜中：大きな床下空間｜下：一部屋に合わせて収納をつくり、可能な限り広がりのあるワンルームに｜Before: Dismantling the partition walls, ceiling, and half of the floor. During: The large underfloor area. After: A storage area was created to fit one part of the floor in order to make the one-room space as large as possible.

海老塚の段差

The Difference of Ebitsuka

HAMAMATSU | 2011

浜松の展開図

The Development of Hamamatsu

HAMAMATSU | 2012

en: art of nexus

上：改修中の物件から建材を回収。
中：壁紙は重ね、フローリングは円形にカット、レンガはすりつぶされた。
下：仏教の世界観を表す曼荼羅の形式にはめ込む。
Before: Salvaging materials from a building under renovation.
During: We overlapped the wallpaper, cut a circle into the floor, and crushed the bricks.
After: Then we used these materials to create a mandala, representing the Buddhist cosmology.

Padiglione Giappone Biennale Architettura 2016

板屋町の壁紙

The Wallpaper of Itayamachi

HAMAMATSU | 2012

「板屋町の壁紙」では、オフィス用のバーチカルブラインドを壁紙として、編み込むようにやや特殊な方法で用いているが、その下地である間柱(まばしら)と胴縁(どうぶち)の構成は、極めて一般的なものである。既存の構法や仕組みを積極的に用いながら、ほんのわずかな慣習からのずれを用いている。「神久呂の屋根」は、老朽化した門の建て替え計画で、既存の門の扉が大きく重いこと、また雨によって腐朽が進んでいることの、解決が求められた。近年開発された高性能な金物を用いる一方、日本の伝統的な薬医門(やくいもん)の形式を参照することで、門のアップデートを図った。現代における地域性とは、伝統的な構法や、地産の高品質な材料のみに宿っているのではない。また、高度な工業製品や、規格化された既製品も、忌み嫌う対象ではない。それらをフラットに、その場の状況に応じて取捨選択しながら、新しい文脈を紡いでいくことこそが地域性をつくる。

In *The Wallpaper of Itayamachi*, we used a somewhat unique weaving method to make vertical blinds into wallpaper, but the structure of the columns and furring strips that made up the underfloor were extremely regular. While proactively using existing methods and mechanisms, we employ approaches that differ very slight from the norm. In *The Roof of Kakuro*, a project to replace a decrepit gate, our approach was determined by the fact that the existing doors were big and heavy, and they had also begun to decay due to the rain. While making use of high-performance hardware that has been developed in recent years, we referred to the form of *yakuimon*, a traditional style of Japanese gate, in order to update the design. Contemporary locality is not merely based on traditional construction methods and locally produced, high-quality materials. Nor are advanced industrial products and standardized readymade goods objects of loathing. By unemotionally choosing the correct thing to match the circumstances in a place, you can create a locality that manifests a new context.

上：オフィスのバーチカルブラインド｜中：施工現場を展覧会や、フリーの工房としても運営した｜下：編み込まれた壁紙｜Before: Vertical blinds in the office.｜During: The space was also used as a construction site exhibition and a free studio.｜After: Interwoven pieces of wallpaper.

上：建て替え前の門｜中：敷地内の伝統的な形式の正門｜下：屋根は銅葺きで、酸化することで周辺と馴染む｜Before: The old gate before it was replaced.｜During: The traditional form of the main gate on the lot.｜After: The roof is topped with copper, which gradually blends in with the surroundings as it is oxidized.

403architecture [dajiba]

098-

神久呂の屋根

The Roof of Kakuro

HAMAMATSU | 2014

しました。なぜなら、「モノ」の縁についての取り組みであれば、「モノ」そのものよりも、その「捉え方」をもっていったほうが、よりクリアに「縁」について伝えることができると考えたためです。

そういうわけで、ヴェネチアン・グラスの廃ガラスを、スランピングと呼ばれる手法で再成形し、石材のようなピースを作成し、それを用いてアーチ状のベンチをつくっています。ヴェネチアの象徴的な風景である「橋」が、まさにあちらとこちらを繋ぐ「縁」であることに拠っています。ヴェネチアの伝統的な技術、流動的な素材、歴史的な風景といった「モノ」にまつわる縁を、捉えようとしています。

Interview | 09 | 403 architecture [dajiba]

Q | How did you approach the theme of *en* in this exhibition?

We're based in Hamamatsu, a city in Shizuoka Prefecture, and the majority of the projects we have been involved with have been part of an effort to develop a design practice that is closely connected to a specific area by, for example, concentrating on things that are within a kilometer radius of our office. As we usually think of architecture in terms of a quite concrete, direct relationship between people and things, the theme of *en* (connection) was actually quite familiar to us.

Except that when you consider *en* as a relationship, there are relationships between all kinds of things, so it can be applied to anything. Since one of the categories was *en* as it applied to things, we thought we would try to suggest how things could be discovered and placed in a new context in our projects.

In order to do this, instead of focusing on a single project, we created an exhibit examining how we handled things in several different projects. To be more precise, we focused on ten projects using a series of photographs illustrating three stages: before, during, and after. For example, in The

富塚の天井

The Ceiling of Tomitsuka

HAMAMATSU | 2012

「富塚の天井」は農園芸用の遮光・防風メッシュを用いている。室内にも室外にも同様に天井として張られ、それぞれ人工照明と自然光とを柔らかに拡散させている。「鍵屋の敷地」は、小規模な店舗のインテリアにもかかわらず、標準的な住宅1軒分の柱材が用いられている。

前者は、地域の気候的特徴に由来する風景の特徴と、日当たりの良くない庭とテラスという局所的な条件を結び付けたものである。後者は、良質な木材を抱える山々を抱えながら、出荷先が不足しているという地域の産業的な問題と、小規模の物販店の参入障壁を下げるための運営形式とを、架橋したものである。両者とも、ある一定の範囲に見られる地域的な特性と、個別ながらも普遍性のある問題とを、特定のマテリアルによって関連付けている。コンテクストとして捉えられる射程を、マテリアルが結んでいく。

In *The Ceiling of Tomitsuka*, we made use of lightproof, windproof agricultural mesh. By using it as a ceiling both inside and outside, the material gently diffused both artificial and natural light. Despite the small interior of the shop in *The Site of Kagiya*, we used the standard number of columns for a house.
The design of the original building was related to special landscape features, derived from climatic conditions in the area, and topical conditions such as a garden and terrace with poor lighting conditions. In the new design, we bridged a local industrial problem in which despite being blessed with mountains containing good-quality lumber, there was a shortage of buyers, and a management system designed to lower the barriers to entering small-scale stores. We came up with materials to deal with both the local qualities and problems that were at once specific and universal. The material is connected to the scope that can be grasped as a context.

100-

403 architecture [dajiba]

鍵屋の敷地

The Site of Kagiya

HAMAMATSU | 2014

Floor of Atsumi, there is a photograph of the ceiling being torn out and exposed ceiling joists, a photograph of them being cut into thin pieces and layered on the floor, and a photograph of the finished floor. In addition, not only is the actual process divided up temporally, the display also deals with things as reference sources. For example, in *The Ceiling of Tomitsuka*, this includes the windbreak nets installed in the fields, and the typical Hamamatsu landscape, an area known for its strong, dry Enshu winds.

We also thought that rather than simply introducing various projects from the past as a way of exploring the *en* of things, it would be better to display real things. Instead of just bringing lumber remnants and mockups from a project, it seemed better to produce an actual object on site using materials from Venice to show how things develop in direct relation to a place. If the idea was to deal with the *en* between things, it seemed like bringing the approach rather than the things themselves would more clearly convey this concept.

As a result, we reshaped Venetian glass waste using a technique called slumping, creating a stone-like material, which we used to make an arch-shaped bench. A bridge, one of Venice's most famous landmarks, can truly serve as the foundation for *en* in many different places. In this project, we attempted to capture the *en* of things as exemplified by Venice's traditional techniques, fluid materials, and historical landscapes.

雑多なモノを
無数の時間の表象として
等価に捉えつつ、
緻密に織り上げる

Treating Various Things Equally
as Symbols of Multiple Times,
and Minutely Weaving
Them Together

青木弘司建築設計事務所

Koji Aoki Architects

調布の家

House in Chofu

TOKYO | 2014

家にはそこに住まう家族によって生きられた時間がある。だが、リノベーションでは、そうした時間をまったく排除するか、柱や梁などの既存のエレメントを部分的に生かすことによって標本化してしまうケースがほとんどである。「調布の家」は、あらゆる雑多なモノが孕みもつ無数の時間を等価に捉えながら、それらの膨大なモノの関係性を緻密に織り上げるように設計することで、すべての時間を一元化せず、バラバラのまま並存させようとしている。この時に住み手は、持続的に空間にかかわりながら、その無数の関係性を再編し、断続的に立ち現れるシーンとして受容していく。生きられる空間とは、その場の質がそこに住まう人間によって日々刻々と変化する空間である。そして、この時に定着される多様な質の広がりによって、空間の豊かさが担保される。そのような空間は、自由であり、新しい発見に満ち溢れていて、人間の生き方を新たに枠付けていく。

Living times vary depending on the family that lives in a house. In most cases, a renovation project completely eliminates these times, or samples them by making partial use of existing elements in the house such as columns and beams. While approaching the infinite times contained in all kinds of different things in an equal manner, *House in Chofu* was designed to carefully create interconnections between this massive number of things. In this way, it allows all of the different times to coexist without reducing them to a single dimension. While maintaining a link to the space, the resident reorganizes these countless interconnections, accepting them as scenes that intermittently arise. The qualities of a living space are constantly changing depending on the people who live there. And the wide range of qualities attached to a given time ensure the richness of the space. This type of space, free and full of new discoveries, provides a new framework for the resident's own way of life.

敷地は東京郊外の住宅地で、近くに大学もあることから、木造のアパートも目立つ。この計画では、要素を削ぎ落していくのではなく、むしろ、新旧が分からないぐらい、あらゆるモノを混ぜ合わせている。それは、周囲の木造のアパートが建ち並ぶ風景と同様に「小さいモノが混在する」状態そのものとも言える。たとえば、合板や塗装、ビニルクロスなどで断片的に仕上げられた内壁と、窓からのぞく隣家のパッチワーク状の外装材が連続的に捉えられるように、モノの集合の密度によって、内外を等価に扱いたいと考えた。

The lot is located in a residential area in the suburbs of Tokyo and wooden apartment buildings stand out, in part because there is a university nearby. In this plan, rather than eliminating various elements, we set out to combine all kinds of things until it was no longer possible to distinguish between old and new. This was a clear effort to create a mixture of small things like the surrounding landscape, which is made up of rows of wooden apartments. Using a dense concentration of things designed to make a visual connection between the inside walls, which were finished with fragments of plywood, paint, and vinyl cloth, and the patchwork-style cladding of the house next door, we wanted to treat the exterior and interior equally.

site plan
1:2000

「調布の家」では、あらゆる雑多なモノが、価値の優劣なく断片的に併置されている。たとえば、屋根裏部屋で使われていたデコラティブな既製品の開きドアは、2階の納戸の扉に転用された。レバーハンドルを回転して固定することで引手とし、取り外された丁番の跡を残したまま引戸に変更され、ラワン合板の素地の壁に即物的に取り付けられている。ラワン合板の素地という、どちらかというと粗野な材料を背景に、複製品がモンタージュされている。

既存の柱や梁といった部位は、墨付けによる記号やメモ書きを残しつつ、その一つひとつをペーパーで磨き上げ、新設した材料とのテクスチャーや色味の差異を調整している。また、既存のアルミサッシの周囲の外壁は解体され、ガラスの壁を設けて開口を拡張している。サッシの付枠は再塗装する程度で放置されているが、枠と取り合う壁の仕上げ厚を変えることで、枠の見込みも相対的に変わり、その存在感が適度に強調されている。屋根裏に新設したトップライトの一部は、天井懐内の立ち上がり部分を設置したあとに、既存の天井下地を復元している。

2階のキッチンは1階に移設し、ステンレス製の膳板(ぜんいた)が取り付けられた出窓だけが、唐突に2階のリビングルームに取り残されている。これとは別の場所に新設したサッシ回りには、同様のステンレス板を張った柱型を現すことで、出窓の膳板の素材感を相対化している。

In *House in Chofu*, a wide range of things was juxtaposed without any concern for their respective value. For example, the readymade, decorative door that had been used in the attic was moved to the storage room on the second floor, and by turning or setting the lever handle as a knob, we turned it into a sliding door using the traces of the hinges that remained there, and attaching it to the lauan plywood wall surface in a utilitarian manner. The readymade door creates a kind of montage, with the plywood wall as a rather rough background. Marks and notes were made in ink to record the position of existing columns and beams, and each one was polished with paper, creating different textures and colors that

↓

104-

House in Chofu Koji Aoki Architects

plan 1:400

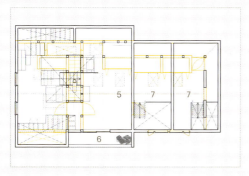

attic floor

first floor

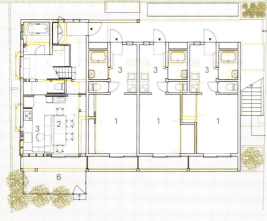

ground floor

1 living room　5 attic
2 dining room　6 balcony
3 kitchen　　　7 loft
4 bedroom

インタビュー｜10｜青木弘司建築設計事務所

Q｜「en（縁）」というテーマについてどのように考えて参加されましたか？

われわれが住宅を設計する場合、施主と何度も打ち合わせを重ね、あらゆる事柄を厳密に計画しても、しょせんそれは想定に過ぎず、引き渡しの時点で書き終えられたシナリオは、実際に生活が始まると、住み手の経験によって書き換えられていきます。このように、計画と経験の間には、ある宿命的なジレンマがあるわけです。そして、このような時間的な断絶を無批判に受け入れることは、ある時点のみに対して最適化された事柄が、住み手の生活を先導してしまうような、ある種の閉塞感を助長させてしまうことにもなりかねない。

このような日々の葛藤から、「今現在」が絶対化し、それが創作の根拠になっている昨今の状況を懐疑的に見ています。「今現在」に最適化された空間は、過去と切断され、未来にも生き延びられないのではないかと思っているからです。「今現在」に創作の主題を見出すのではなく、建築の創作に時間性を召還し、その射程を再考することで、過去を標本化せず、それを意味のあるものとして捉え直し、同時に「今現在」が持続していくものとして未来を位置付けなければならないのではないでしょうか。

そこで、今回展示する「調布の家」では、今までの時間も、これからの時間もバラバラのまま並存させるために、空間を形づくる、あらゆる雑多なモノを無数の時間の表象として等価に捉えながら、それらの膨大なモノとモノの関係性、つまり、「モノの縁」を緻密に織り上げるように設計しています。この時に住み手は、持続的に空間にかかわりながら、その無数の「モノの縁」を再編し、断続的に立ち現れるシーンとして受容していきます。このように、その場の質が人間の主体性によって日々刻々と変化するような、いつまでもみずみずしく新鮮な、冗長性に溢れた空間を設計したいと思っています。

先の見えにくい状況ですが、今を生きる建築家と

section 1:100

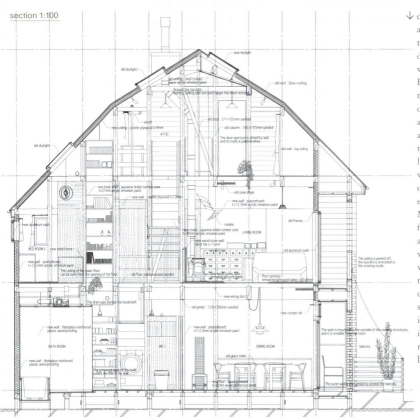

could be used as new materials. In addition, the exterior wall around the existing aluminum sashes was dismantled, and a glass wall with wider openings was installed. Except for repainting the sashes, they were left as they were, and by changing the thickness of the wall around the sashes, we altered their appearance, and slightly accentuated their presence. After part of the top light, newly installed in the attic, was attached to the rising section of the ceiling cavity, the base of the existing ceiling was restored. Moreover, the kitchen was moved from the second to the first floor, and only the bay window, fitted with a stainless-steel window board was left as an abrupt presence in the second-floor living room. By creating a column covered with the same type of stainless-steel plating in a different place around a newly installed sash, it relativized the material quality of the window board around the bay window.

House in Chofu　Koji Aoki Architects

ラワン合板仕上げの間仕切り壁は、その高さに応じて繊維方向を交互に並べて突き付けることで、後から場当たり的に付け足されたように見せている。また、そのスケールを家具などに同調させ、近傍の木枠や手摺の見付けに合わせるように壁厚を極力抑えながら、既存の壁から棒材を渡して固定している。石膏ボードの壁も、ただ立て掛けられているように見せるために、その端部や隣接する部材との取り合い部分の納まりには特に気を使い、3種類の見切り縁を併用している。階段などは、各部のデザインを変えつつ全体を白く塗り込めて、トップライトの直下に再配置することで、周囲から少し浮き上がる存在に仕立てている。↓

106-

して、どのような創作の主題を設定することができるのだろうかと日頃から考えています。今われわれの実践の舞台は、いわゆる大文字の建築が信頼を失いつつある社会です。ひょっとすると、「縁」というテーマを設定することが、少しナイーブな態度のように受け取られるかも知れませんが、それでも、さまざまな社会の問題に真摯に向き合うわれわれの実践を俯瞰していくと、今この時代が要求する創作の主題を探り当てることができるはずです。そして、この展覧会を通して浮かび上がった創作の主題から、未来に対して開かれた、建築の新しい自律性が紡がれていくことを、私自身も期待しています。

Interview | 10 | Koji Aoki Architects

Q | How did you approach the theme of *en* in this exhibition?

When we design a house, we have many meetings with the client, and even if we rigorously design all kinds of elements, these are nothing more than assumptions at the beginning. The final scenario at the time that we hand over the house to the client is rewritten according to the residents' experiences when they actually start living there. Thus, between the plan and the experience, there is destined to be a dilemma. Accepting this temporal discontinuity uncritically tends to promote a sense of closure in which conditions that are only optimal at a given point in time take precedence over the residents' lives.

Out of this daily conflict, the present becomes absolute and the recent conditions that formed a basis for creating the building come to be viewed with skepticism. This is due to the fact that a space that is optimized for the present cannot be severed from the past or survive in the future. Rather than searching for a subject to create in the present, temporality is summoned back to architecture, and by reconsidering its range, it is recaptured as something meaningful without sampling the past. At the same time, it also seems

↓吹き抜け部分の手摺は、隣り合う部分で部材や仕上げを変えながら、本工事として設える部分と住み手のDIYに委ねる部分が判然としないようにしている。これに加えて、壁や天井の仕上げに関しては、石膏ボードを白く塗装する、合板の素地を現す、既存の仕上げを剥がす、そのまま残すというように、おおよそ4種類の仕上げを注意深く混在させている。

Alternating the direction of the fiber in accordance with the height of the partition wall, which was finished with lauan plywood, made it look as if it had been added later in a haphazard way. And by making it the same scale as the furniture, and crossing and affixing bars from the existing wall to it, we did our best to control the wall's thickness to make it match the appearance of the wooden frames and handrails nearby. As the plaster-board walls also look as if they are leaning, we took special care to adjust the proportions of the edges, and the adjoining and conflicting parts, combining the three types of parting edges. For the stairs and other areas, we altered the design of each part and painted the whole thing white, and by relocating it directly under the top light, we made it seem to rise up slightly from its surroundings. Though we altered the materials and finish of adjacent parts in the handrails in the stairwell, it was hard to distinguish which parts had been newly installed in this project and which ones were from the residents' own DIY projects.
In addition, by painting the plaster board white, leaving the surface of the plywood exposed, stripping off the existing finish and leaving it in that state, we created an intriguing combination of four different finishes for the walls and ceiling.

House in Chofu | Koji Aoki Architects

necessary to locate the present in the future as something that can be sustained.

Therefore, in *House in Chofu*, our contribution to the exhibition, we have shaped the space to allow a variety of different times up to the present to exist separately but simultaneously. And by approaching a variety of different things equally as symbols of many different times, we have designed a relationship between this immense number of things, or intricately interwoven the *en* of these things. In this situation, while maintaining a link with the space, the residents reedit the countless *en* of things and accept them as intermittently emerging scenes. In this way, we hope to design spaces in which the qualities of the place are constantly changing through people's activities, and also remain fresh, new, and filled with a diffuse quality.

Though it is difficult to judge what might happen in the future, as architects living in the current era, we consider how to determine the subject of our work on a daily basis. The stage for our practice is a society that has lost faith in architecture in the most literal sense of the word. Though the use of *en* as a theme might be seen as a slightly naïve approach, in surveying our practice as we sincerely attempt to confront a variety of problems facing society, you should be able to detect creative subjects that are critical to the present era. We also anticipate that the subjects that emerge in this exhibition will lead to a greater openness in the future and a new sense of autonomy in architecture.

The En of

House for Seven People Mio Tsuneyama / mnm

Yokohama Apartments Osamu Nishida + Erika Nakagawa

LT Josai Naruse Inokuma Architects

Apartments with a Small Restaurant Naka Architects' Studio

Guest House in Takaoka Nousaku Architects

House at Komazawa Park Mizuki Imamura + Isao Shinohara / miCo.

15A House Levi Architecture

Boundary Window Shingo Masuda + Katsuhisa Otsubo Architects

The Floor of Atsumi, etc. 403architecture [dajiba]

House in Chofu Koji Aoki Architects

Projects in Kamiyama BUS

Umaki Camp Beat Shrine dot architects

地域の縁

Locality

日本では、地方は過疎の状態にある。中央からの資本投下は乏しく、人口は減少していく。かつて栄えた商業地域では客足が遠のき、閉鎖された店舗も多い。停滞した雰囲気が地方都市には漂っている。

———

だが、2010年代になると、過疎の惰性をわずかながらも揺るがす動きが、密かに起こるようになる。本展示の神山と小豆島は、その中でも特に興味深い事例である。いずれにも共通するのは、まず、アートとの接点である。アーティスト・イン・レジデンスの試みが、外の世界を地域へと招き入れていくきっかけになる。地域の人びとは、アーティストとの交流を通じ、自分たちでも何かやってみようと思うようになる。そして、この機運を持続させていこうとする、キーパーソンがいる。彼らは外から人を呼び入れ仕事の場を紹介するというだけでなく、外からの人を地域の人と出会わせ、その交流から、人が集まる場をつくる。さらに、働くこと、食べること、語らうことといった生活の基本の支えとなる、地に足の着いた地道な生活空間をつくり出していくことを手助けする。IT関連（ウェブデザインやデータ管理など）の仕事、家具、靴、農業、プロダクトデザインなど、さまざまな仕事の担い手が集まっていく。これらの試みを神山の人たちは「創造的過疎」と呼び、過疎に前向きな態度で向き合っている。

———

「地域の縁」の土台において成り立っている建築群は、いずれも簡素で、声高ではない。川や樹木、街並みの中にあって、静かに、落ち着いてたたずんでいる。だが、それはただ周辺環境との調和といった状態を意味しない。そこで生活している人たちが集ま

り、仕事をし、食事をするという営みを誘発し、定着させ、支えることの条件となる空間性が、建築の個々において実現されている。建築家自身が、地域において生じてきた生活の縁の中に住み着く中で、自らの身体感覚の水準でつかみとった集まりの潜在空間を建築として形式化した所産である。

———

以上の建築群が提示するのは、次のことである。人間生活は、生活空間の連関の中で営まれている。多数の空間が、ひとつの全体へと統合されるのではなく、ゆるやかに交錯し、連関していく。生活空間は、ひとつの仮想された全体の一部として存在するのではない。個々においてまとまりをもち、独自のたたずまい、奥行きをたたえた状態にあるものとして、つくり出され、成り立っている。ただし、おのおのの生活空間は、自足し、切り離されるのではなく、他の空間と、区別されつつ連関する。生活の場がたたえるたたずまい、気配は、個物の総和というよりはむしろ、相互連関において生じている。そして、人間生活には、建築がかかわってくる。建築は、ただ建築物を建てる営みに限定されない。それは生活の場をつくり出す営みの根底にある。

[MS]

Japan's regions outside the major metropolitan areas are becoming depopulated. Capital investment from the center is running short, and the population is declining. What were once prosperous commercial districts now attract few customers, and many stores have shut. An air of stagnation floats over regional cities.

From 2010 on, however, movements to shake up, even slightly, the inertia associated with depopulation have been quietly occurring. The examples from Kamiyama and Shodo Island are particularly interesting. What they share is, first, their connection with art. Artist-in-residence programs are occasions for inviting the outside world into a locality. The people in that locality, through interacting with the artist, come to think that they themselves might try to do something. And key persons who will try to keep up that momentum appear. They want to go beyond inviting people from outside and giving them a place to work to generating encounters between people from outside and people in that locality, and, from their interactions, creating a place where people will gather. In addition, they contribute to creating simple, straightforward living spaces rooted in the region that will sustain the fundamentals of life: working, eating, conversing. These spaces will attract people involved in all sorts of work: IT-related work (in web design or data management, for example), furniture or shoemaking, farming, product design. The people of Kamiyama called these efforts "creative depopulation" addressing depopulation with a positive attitude.

simple and anything but showy. They are quiet, composed presences surrounded by rivers, trees, townscapes. But harmonizing with the surrounding environment is not the whole story. Their spatial qualities, a condition for people living there to gather, work, eat, settle there, support it, are realized through the individual buildings. The architect, living within connections to lifestyles that have arisen in the locality, creates buildings that are the fruit of giving form to potential spaces grasped through his or her level of somesthesis or bodily sensibility.

What these groups of buildings suggest is that human lives take place in connections to living spaces. Multiple spaces are not fused into a single whole but gently mingle and connect. Living spaces do not exist as one part of one hypothetical whole. They are created and stand as things, each of which has coherence, that stand on its own and is full of depth. But each living space is not self sufficient and cut off; each is linked with other spaces, yet separate from them. A residence filled with living spaces, the signs, rather than the sum of the individual parts, arises from mutual relationships. Architecture permeates human life. Architecture is not just building buildings. Architecture is building loci for living, places that become the nexus of human life.   [MS]

-113   Groups of buildings, rising on sites with *en* with the region are

BUS
BUS
神山町プロジェクト
Projects in Kamiyama

TOKUSHIMA | 2010–

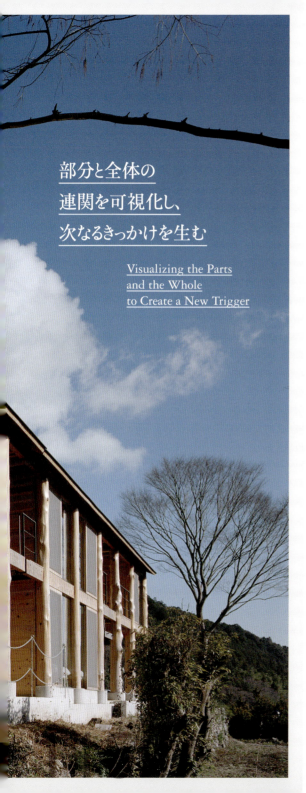

部分と全体の連関を可視化し、次なるきっかけを生む

Visualizing the Parts and the Whole to Create a New Trigger

徳島県の中山間地域に位置する神山町は、全国に点在する、似たような地勢の場所と同様に、人口減少、過疎化・高齢化が進む町である。しかし1999年から続いているアーティスト・イン・レジデンスや近年見られるサテライトオフィスの増加によって、町民、移住者、来訪者などさまざまな人が行き交う町となり、注目を集めている。

町家を改修した「ブルーベアオフィス神山」、古民家を東京に本社のある企業のサテライトオフィスに改修した「えんがわオフィス」「KOYA」、地場産業の林業を活用して丸太材を柱に用いたゲストハウス「WEEK神山」などの施設は、この神山町で2010年からつくられたプロジェクト群である。いずれも町で発生している個々のさまざまな活動と地域との関係を取りもつインフラのように計画された。これらにおいては、成長時代の、マスを対象としたインフラではなく、個の振る舞いに目を向けて、個から発せられるダイナミズムが地域のエネルギーへと繋がる関係性をつくり出すためのインフラのかたちが模索されている。

Like many other places in similar areas across the country, Kamiyama-cho, located in a mountainous region of Tokushima Prefecture, is a town with an aging and decreasing population. But due to the marked increase in artist-in-residence programs and satellite offices since 1999, the town has recently attracted many kinds of people (local residents, new arrivals, travelers), and become a topic of discussion. Facilities such as *Blue Bear Office Kamiyama*, housed in a renovated *machiya* townhouse; *ENGAWA Office*, an old house renovated to serve as a satellite office for a Tokyo-based company; *KOYA*; and *WEEK Kamiyama*, a guest house with columns made of logs from the local forestry industry, are all part of a project that was launched in Kamiyama in 2010. They were designed to function as infrastructure that would create a link between various specific activities that have emerged in the town and the local region. Instead of infrastructure that targets the masses in a growth period, the facilities focus on individual behaviors in order to form a relationship in which the dynamism of individuals connects with regional vitality.

徳島県名西郡神山町は、市街地から車で40分ほどに位置する、人口6,000人ほどの過疎化・高齢化の進む中山間地域の町である。ここでは現地NPO法人グリーンバレーによって、20年ほど前から「アーティスト・イン・レジデンス」「ワーク・イン・レジデンス」などの取り組みが行われ、その成果が町づくりの先進事例として注目を集めている。そんな中、近年この町にサテライトオフィスを構える企業が相次いで現れている。BUSはこの町において、移住者支援のための空き家改修や進出企業のための施設整備を手がけており、すでに7つの建築が竣工している。また、空家改修を行うワークショップ、フィールドワーク、リサーチなどの企画運営を行ったりと、設計・建設行為のみならず、さまざまな角度から町とのかかわりを楽しんでいる。

Kamiyama-cho, Nishi-gun, Tokushima Prefecture, is a town with an aging and decreasing population of 6,000 that is located about 40 minutes by car from the closest urban area. A local NPO called Green Valley began organizing artist- and worker-in-residence programs some 20 years ago, earning the group widespread acclaim as a pioneering example of town planning. In recent years, a succession of companies has set up satellite offices in the town. BUS runs a facility to help new companies make inroads and renovate vacant houses for people who have just moved to the area. The organization has already completed seven construction projects. It also runs workshops dealing with renovation, fieldwork, and research, and besides being involved with design and construction, it deals with the town in a variety of different ways.

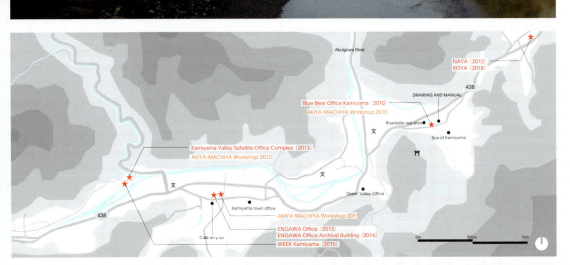

116–

Projects in Kamiyama   BUS

神山バレーサテライト
オフィスコンプレックス

Kamiyama Valley Satellite Office Complex

TOKUSHIMA | 2013

縫製工場をシェアオフィスに改修した計画。この町の特徴である人の流動性の高さに着目し、ガラス間仕切りとしてお互いの姿が見渡せるようにした。初回改修は工事を最小限に留め、その後も手を入れる「成長するオフィス」として計画されている。

Renovation project to convert a garment factory into a shared office space. Focusing on the highly fluid character of the people in the town, glass partitions were created to give people a sweeping view of each other. In the first renovation, construction was kept to a bare minimum in line with a plan for an expanding office that could be modified later.

―117

インタビュー | 11 | BUS

Q |「en(縁)」というテーマについてどのように考えて参加されましたか？

伊藤 | 本展のステートメントに「社会は大きな転換期を迎えている」との言葉がありますが、何が転換しているのか。私は「部分と全体の関係」ではないかと考えています。かつての成長期には社会の全体像がイメージしやすく、そこで共有された規範や仕組みを部分に向けてブレイクダウンするという関係が理解しやすかったのではないでしょうか。しかし現在は、部分からのボトムアップも活況ですし、とはいえ全体の仕組みが力を失っているわけでもなく、その関係性はもっと複雑で、ひとつのイメージでは把握できません。神山町は、日本の「部分の末端」のような町ですが、ここでの出来事は日本国内に留まらず世界各地から注目を集めていて、新しい部分と全体の関係のあり方が感じられる場所です。それを「縁」という言葉で捉え直してみると、より具体的な連関が見えてくるのではないかと思います。

須磨 | 神山町での活動は極私的な「縁」の連鎖からなっています。私自身はニューヨーク在住時に妻同士の交流から紹介された坂東幸輔との出会いから活動が始まり、私を訪ねて神山に遊びに来た高校の同級生はここに惚れ込んで自身の会社のサテライトオフィスを設置し、いまや十数件ある内の1号店です。こうした「縁」を可視化し、次に繋がるきっかけを生み出すことがわれわれの役割だと思っています。

坂東 | 神山町と出合ったきっかけはリーマンショックでした。世界中のどんな設計事務所にでも就職できると思ってハーバード大学を修了しましたがすぐにリーマンショックが起き、ニューヨークで2年間無職を経験しました。古民家に1万円で住めるならアルバイトをしながら建築家を目指すのでは、というような思いで神山町を訪れ、その時の出合いが「ブルーベアオフィス神山」の改修に繋がっています。世界的金融危機を体験し、大きな組織に頼るのではなく、自分の手の届く範囲で活動したいと思うようになりました。これまでのや

WEEK神山

WEEK Kamiyama

TOKUSHIMA | 2015

A block ground floor　　　　　　　　　B block ground floor　　　　　　　　　　　　　plan 1:250

1 dormitory
2 twin room
3 piloti

Projects in Kamiyama BUS

118–

来町者のための宿泊施設。計画地は山や川、空、集落など、町の美しい風景が一望できる場所で、この風景を満喫するために、環境の中に放り出されてしまうような体験をもたらす建物とした。筋交いや壁などの耐震要素によって眺望が阻まれるのを防ぐため、350φの丸太柱を利用した木造ラーメン構造としている。350φの丸太柱は、一般的な木材流通市場では手に入らないが、かつて林業で栄えた神山町の山林から木材を伐採し、柱材として利用している。産地に近いという特性が、流通の合理性から導かれるものとは違う建物の形を実現している。

Lodging facility for visitors to the town. The site affords a view of the town's beautiful scenery, including mountains, rivers, the sky, and other villages. To make the most of this, the building was designed to create the sensation of being thrown out into the environment. To avoid obstructing the view with earthquake-resistant elements such as struts and walls, we created a laminated wood structure made up of log columns with a diameter of 350 mm. These columns are not generally available at the wood market, but we obtained them from the local forest (Kamiyama-cho was once a prosperous lumber town) to use in the project. Due to our proximity to the production area, rational distribution helped us realize a different form of architecture.

り方では通用しないという私と同じような思いをした人は世界中に少なくないのではないでしょうか。転換の兆候は私的な気づきの中にあると思います。

須磨｜「えんがわオフィス」は古民家を改修した最先端のオフィスというひとつのモデルとして、多くの企業がこの町にサテライトオフィスを構えるきっかけとなり、またこの設計が古民家改修への異なる手法を模索した「KOYA」の設計へと繋がっています。

伊藤｜部分と全体について考えることは、単なるコンテクストへの考察のみならず、たとえば「WEEK神山」では柱材を町の山から伐り出したりと、建築のつくられ方にも変化をもたらしています。このような建築のあり方は、これからの時代に向けたヒントになり得るのではないかと思います。

Interview | 11 | BUS

Q | How did you approach the theme of *en* in this exhibition?

Ito | The statement about this exhibition included the phrase, "Society is approaching an important turning point," and that made me wonder what exactly was changing. I decided it might be the relationship between the parts and the whole. It seems to me that during previous growth periods, it was easy to envision a total picture of society that could be broken down into common criteria and parts of the mechanism. Today, however, it has become feasible to work with parts from the bottom up, and at the same time, the mechanism as a whole hasn't lost any of its power. The relationship is more complex and can no longer be understood with a single image. Kamiyama-cho is a town that is on the tip of one part of Japan, but what we did there received attention not only from people all over the country but from countries all over the world. This was a place where it was possible to sense a new relationship between the parts and the

えんがわオフィス
ENGAWA Office
TOKUSHIMA | 2013

東京に本社をもつ企業のサテライトオフィス。築80年ほどの民家(母屋、蔵、納屋の3棟)をオフィスにコンバージョンする計画。2013年の竣工後、2014年にアーカイブ棟を新築して現在の姿に至っている。田舎の民家で東京の企業の社員が働くという出来事を町に定着させるため、外壁をガラス張りにして中の人びとが外から見えるようになっている。母屋はガラスの回りに大きな縁側を配し、建物周辺に人が留まるバッファーを設けている。敷地境界は隣地に対して開かれていて、近隣住民が自由に行き交い、オフィス前の広場は子供たちの遊び場にもなっている。これらのさまざまな人びとの関係が、縁側を介してつくり出されている。

The satellite office of a Tokyo-based company. The project called for an 80-year-old house (made up of three wings: the main house, a storehouse, and a storage room) to be converted into an office. After it was completed in 2013, an archive wing was newly built in 2014, leading to the building's present appearance. To help convey the idea that the employees were working in this rural house, we created a glass exterior wall, making the people inside visible from the outside. And by adding a large veranda around the glass in the main building,

plan 1:200

1 work space
2 kitchen

Projects in Kamiyama BUS

120-

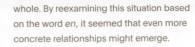

whole. By reexamining this situation based on the word *en*, it seemed that even more concrete relationships might emerge.

Suma | Our project in Kamiyama-cho is a

we created a buffer, so that people would remain on the periphery of the structure. The site's boundary was open to the adjacent lot, allowing the neighbors to move back and forth freely, and the square in front of the office became a playground for children. A variety of interpersonal relationships were created by the veranda.

—121

KOYA/NAYA

KOYA/NAYA

TOKUSHIMA | 2012, 2015

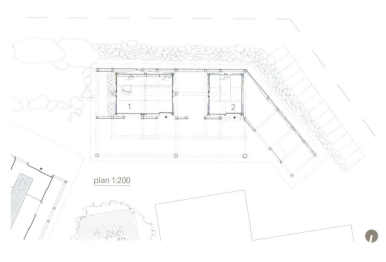

plan 1:200

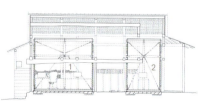

1 work space
2 meeting room

section 1:200

Projects in Kamiyama BUS

122-

東京に本社をもつIT企業のサテライトオフィス。築100年ほど経つ苔むしわびた牛小屋はそのままに、オフィスは内部に間借りするかたちで建っている。鉄骨の構造体は牛小屋に触れてはいないが、大規模災害時には倒壊を防ぐ要石となるよう、牛小屋全体を支えられる強度をもつよう設計されている。他にも地場産の杉と石を使って組み上げた大きなデスクのある「NAYA」、庭の池を眺めながらハンモックの上での作業など、同じ敷地内において思い思いの働き方のできる環境となっている。

The satellite office of a Tokyo-based IT company. The moss-covered cattle shed, built some 100 years old, has retained its original form, and the office now resides inside. Though the steel framework of the shed remains unchanged, the office was designed to be strong and support the shed like a keystone warding off destruction in a massive earthquake. *NAYA*, which contains a large desk built out of locally grown cedar and stones, became an environment that promotes each person's preferred way of working, including laying in a hammock and gazing at the pond in the garden.

ブルーベアオフィス神山

Blue Bear Office Kamiyama

TOKUSHIMA | 2010

Projects in Kamiyama BUS

建築の設計だけでなく地域の住民と多様なかかわりを生み出し将来の町のヴィジョンを共有できるワークショップを行うことは、BUSの活動において重要なものとなっている。2010年に神山町にかかわるきっかけとなった「ブルーベアオフィス神山」では大学生たちと空き家再生のワークショップで改修を行った。その後も、1929年に建てられた劇場「寄井座」を調査し再生案を考えるワークショップや、町内で不要になった家具を再生し「神山バレーサテライトオフィスコンプレックス」の家具を制作するワークショップを行っている。

In addition to architectural design, one of BUS's most important activities is organizing workshops, which help manifest a common vision for the town's future by creating various relationship with local residents. In 2010, *Blue Bear Office Kamiyama*, which was inspired to become involved with Kamiyama-cho, held a renovation workshop in which university students helped restore a vacant house. This was followed by other events, such as a workshop to survey and create a restoration plan for the Yorii-za theatre, which was built in 1929, and a workshop in which furniture that had fallen into disuse in the town was recycled for use in the *Kamiyama Valley Satellite Office Complex*.

chain of extremely private *en*. The project began while I was living in New York. I met Kosuke Bando through our wives, who were already acquainted. And then one of my high school classmates came to visit me in Kamiyama-cho and after falling in love with the place, he set up a satellite office for his company there. It was the first of what now numbers a couple dozen offices. I see our role as visualizing *en* and creating triggers that will lead to the next thing.

Bando | The trigger that led me to Kamiyama-cho was the financial crisis of 2008. I thought that after graduating from Harvard University I would be able to find a job at any architecture firm in the world, but that crisis occurred and I spent two years unemployed in New York. I visited Kamiyama-cho with the idea that I might rent an old house for 10,000 yen a month, and work part-time while trying to make it as an architect. Just at that point, I became involved in renovating *Blue Bear Office Kamiyama*. Having experienced the global financial crisis, I started thinking I wanted to do something within my own reach instead of relying on a big organization. And I figured that there must be quite a few other people like me in the world who could not accept conventional ways of doing things. A promise of change was contained in my own personal realization.

Suma | *ENGAWA Office*, a state-of-the-art office in a renovated house, served as a model, inspiring many other companies to make satellite offices in the town. And this in turn led to the design for *KOYA*, which explored a different method of renovating an old house.

Ito | Thinking about the parts and the whole is more than simply considering the context. For example, in *WEEK Kamiyama*, cutting down timber in the mountains to use as columns changed the way the building was made. I think this type of approach will provide more hints for future generations.

新旧の繋がりを
大切にする
メディアとしての建築

Architecture as a Media
for Carefully Creating
Relationships
between New and Old

ドットアーキテクツ
dot architects

馬木キャンプ
Umaki Camp
SHODOSHIMA | 2013

「馬木キャンプ」と「美井戸(びーと)神社」は、東京から遠く離れた瀬戸内海に浮かぶ小豆島にある。小豆島のような周縁の地域では少子高齢化と人口減少が進んでおり、中央省庁の縦割り行政だけに頼っていては存続が難しい状況にある。というのも、島の日常の暮らしや島が抱えているさまざまな課題は、省庁やセクションの枠を超えて横に繋がっているからである。こうした状況では、島の人びとは強い絆で結ばれたコミュニティを土台にしてお互いを助け合いながら、自分たち自身の手で自律的に地域社会をつくると同時に、島外の人びとと積極的に交流し関係を築いていく必要性がある。「馬木キャンプ」は、建設が簡易な構法によってセルフビルドを可能にするハードと、地域の連帯や交流を促進するためのソフトを同時に提案することで小さな社会実験の場として機能している。「美井戸神社」は地域の風土を大切に考え、また、島の外から人びとが訪れるきっかけとなるシンボルとして機能している。

Umaki Camp and *Beat Shrine* are located on Shodoshima, an island in the Seto Inland Sea far from Tokyo. Outlying areas such as this one are faced with a constantly decreasing birthrate as well as an aging and decreasing population, and relying solely on vertically-segmented government ministries and agencies makes their survival difficult. Moreover, everyday life on Shodoshima and the island's various problems are closely connected in a horizontal manner that transcends traditional government frameworks.
In these circumstances, while taking advance of the strong ties that exist in the community to help each other, there is a necessity for the islanders to create an autonomous regional society with their own hands. At the same time, it is vital that they also develop a proactive approach to exchanges with those outside the island. *Umaki Camp* serves as the site of a small social experiment by simultaneously proposing hardware that can be self-built using a simple construction method and software that promotes regional solidarity and exchange. *Beat Shrine*, carefully created by taking the local climate into account, functions as a symbol to attract visitors from outside.

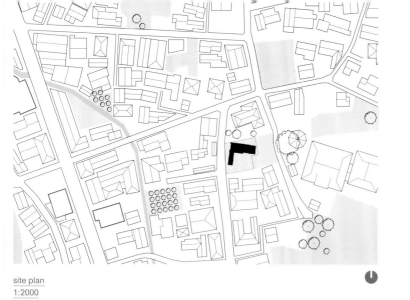

site plan
1:2000

細道と水路と家並みから成る馬木の集落においては、大きくてシンプルな大屋根では目線で感じる集落のスケールと合わない。そこで屋根を小さく5つに分節し、それぞれの仕上げを変えることで威圧感をなくし親しみやすいたたずまいとなるようにした。

In the village of Umaki, made up of narrow roads, water channels, and rows of houses, a large simple roof would not match the scale of the town, in which everything can be experienced through your own sightline. By making a small roof, dividing it into five parts, and finishing each part in a different way, we created an appearance that was meant to eliminate a sense of overwhelming power and encourage a feeling of intimacy.

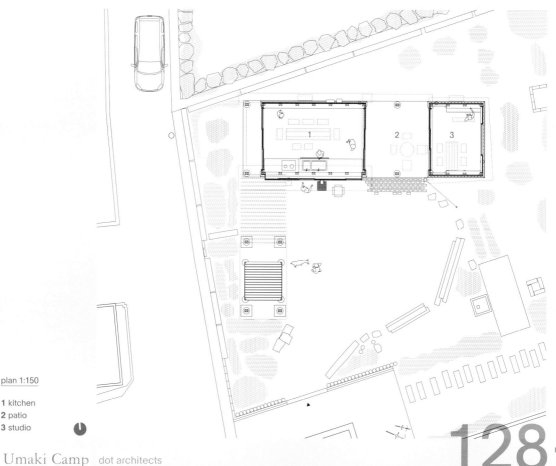

plan 1:150

1 kitchen
2 patio
3 studio

Umaki Camp   dot architects

128-

インタビュー | 12 | ドットアーキテクツ

Q |「en（縁）」というテーマについてどのように考えて参加されましたか？

「馬木キャンプ」と「美井戸神社」は、ふたつの「縁」と関係があります。ひとつは、日常生活での助け合いや共同作業などを通じて地域の方々が長い歴史の中で積み上げてきた「縁」です。もうひとつは、共同体の外からやって来る人や情報と繋がりを結ぶ、新しい「縁」です。

ふたつの「縁」は、小豆島が橋のない離島であることに関係があると思います。小豆島は海に囲まれているので、地縁や血縁が強く、住民の皆さんの地域に対する思いや住民同士の関係性は濃密であると同時に、瀬戸内海の要所に位置しており、霊場でもあるので、外からやって来るさまざまな人や物資、情報に対して寛容さをもっています。ですからこのふたつのプロジェクトでは、その場所にもともと培われた必然の「縁」と、たまたま出合って培われる偶然の「縁」の両方を大切に考えました。

「馬木キャンプ」では、構造家の満田衛資さんと考案したセルフビルドを可能にする構法によって、高度な技術を使わず、手で持ち運べる材料でできているので、建設現場に非専門家のさまざまな人たちとのかかわりしろをつくり出すことができます。同時に人と人、人と町を繋げる媒介となるように、動物、食、ラジオ局、映画、アーカイブというソフトを提案し、地域住民と協働することで新たな発見やアイデアが生まれました。「瀬戸内国際芸術祭2013」の出展作品として建設されましたが、現在も福祉や教育、集いを通じた小さな社会実験の場となり、地域住民の活動や行政の協力によって存続しています。

「美井戸神社」は、ビートたけし氏とヤノベケンジ氏によって制作された「ANGER from the Bottom」という彫刻作品を風雨から守り、地域の風土や自然を大切に考えるためのシンボルとして建設されました。この社は、小豆島町の自治会代表、経済界、地域住民などで構成された「美

建物は、隣人の方が大切に育てていた植物をかわすために、敷地に対して少し振って建てられている。それによって大きな広場や小さな菜園など敷地と建物の間の外部空間を上手く使えるようにした。建物の用途は、5つに分節された屋根に対応してヤギ小屋、藤棚、キッチン、パティオ、スタジオとなっている。既存の集会所と違い、開口部を大きくしているので、建物内での活動と広場や道の活動が互いに認識できる。

To avoid interfering with the vegetables the neighbor was carefully growing, the building was slightly staggered on the lot. This made it possible to skillfully use the outside space between the lot and the building as a large square and vegetable garden. The building's uses, corresponding to the five divisions in the roof, are goat shed, wisteria trellis, kitchen, patio, and studio. Unlike existing assembly rooms, the openings in the building are large, allowing people inside and those in the square and on the road to be aware of each other's activities.

section 1:150

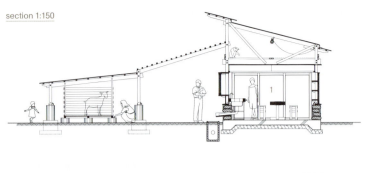

1 kitchen
2 patio
3 studio

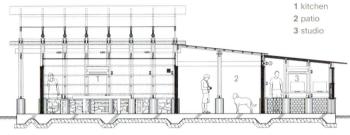

セルフビルドを可能にする現代版の掘立て小屋である。プレカットや熟練の複雑な仕口など、高度な技術は用いず、誰もが建物をつくることにかかわれる構法でできている。柱はヴォイド管を型枠にしたコンクリート基礎に差し込むことで自立し、梁や水平材もすべて直線カットした後、ボルトや釘で固定されている。真っすぐ切る技術と穴を開ける技術があれば棟上げができる。加えて構造がひと目で分かるように仕上げを施すことで、今後の改変や修復を容易にすると同時に、石や焼杉など地域の素材を積極的に使用している。また、各用途によって天井の仕上げを変えることで場所の性格を変えている。たとえばキッチン（下）は、透光性のあるテント幕の屋根から入ってくる光を半透明の天井が拡散し、日中は外部のように明るい。

Umaki Camp　dot architects

130

This contemporary form of hut can be self-built. Without advanced technology such as precutting and complex joints, this construction method enables anyone to erect the building. Void tubes are inserted into a molded concrete foundation to make self-supporting columns, and after cutting all of the beams and horizontal members in straight lines, they are affixed with bolts or nails. If a person has the ability to cut straight and drill holes, they can raise the framework of the building. In addition, the quickly understandable finish of the structure will make future renovations and restorations easy, and encourage the use of local materials such as stone and burned cedar. Moreover, altering the ceiling finish according to its use gives each place a different character. For example, in the kitchen (above), light that is allowed into the space through the translucent tent in the roof is diffused by the semi-transparent ceiling, giving the room a degree of brightness akin to the outside during the daytime.

井戸神社をつくる会」の発足を経て、小豆島の方々から集められたご浄財によって建設へと動き出し、竣工後は「美井戸神社をまもる会」によって維持管理され、島外からも多くの方が訪れる場所となっています。

現在、物や情報が中心から周縁へと広がる構図ではなく、周縁と周縁が、コミュニティとコミュニティがダイレクトに繋がり関係性をつくっていける時代です。もとからある必然の「縁」を大切にしつつ、閉じずに新しくできる偶然の「縁」を受け入れる土台になることが建築に課せられたひとつの役割だと思います。

Interview | 12 | dot architects

Q | How did you approach the theme of *en* in this exhibition?

Umaki Camp and *Beat Shrine* are connected to two kinds of en. The first has accumulated over a long history as local people have helped each other and engaged in cooperative projects in daily life. The second is a new kind of *en*, which creates links with people from outside the community and information.

These two *en* are related to the fact that Shodoshima is an isolated island without any bridges. As the island is surrounded by water, there are strong geographic and family ties, and there is also a strong sense of connection to the local area and between the residents. At the same time, as it is located at a strategic point in the Seto Inland Sea, and is considered to be a sacred place, local residents have an open-minded attitude toward people, goods, and information from outside. So in these two projects, we carefully considered both the inevitable *en* cultivated by the place itself, and the accidental *en* cultivated through chance encounters.

Using a self-built method conceived with the builder Eisuke Mitsuda enabled us to carry the materials manually without

(continues on p.135)

建物と同時に地域の方々とともにいろいろなソフトを考案した。ヤギを地域の方々と一緒に飼うことで(下右)、地域の方々や島外から訪れる人が話すきっかけができたり、ミニFM局を開設することで(下左)、情報の受け手から発信者に変わることができる。夏の間は採れすぎた家庭菜園の野菜を持ち込んでもらい、地域の方や観光客が自由に調理して食べることができる。また、地域の方々だけで短編映画をつくり、野外上映会を行うことで(上)、地域の方々がたくさん集まる機会をつくったり、地域の家に眠っている昔の写真を収集してデジタルアーカイブにしていく試みも行った。

Along with the building, we considered a variety of soft elements with local people. Raising goats with the residents (center) provided a topic of conversation with other people from the area as well as visitors to the island. And by starting a mini-FM station (below), people went from being receivers to transmitters of information. Bringing vegetables from their home gardens (which produce an abundant crop during the summer), local residents and sightseers are free to cook and eat in the space. In addition, locally produced short movies are screened outside (above), other events are planned for people to gather, and a digital archive of old photographs, which had been lying dormant in people's houses, was created.

Umaki Camp / dot architects

ドットアーキテクツ

dot architects

美井戸神社

Beat Shrine

SHODOSHIMA | 2014

小豆島の洞雲山を背後に控え、人びとの生活を支えた井戸の跡地に設置されたビートたけし氏とヤノベケンジ氏による彫刻「ANGER from the Bottom」には、現在の自然と人間の関係に警告を鳴らす意味が込められている。これを雨乞いや治水の神様の依り代として祀る神事が行われたことを契機に社建設の話がもち上がった。「美井戸神社」の形式は神明造や、その起源と言われる弥生時代の建築を参照し、平入（ひらいり）、掘立（ほったて）、棟持柱（むなもちばしら）、矩勾配の切妻屋根ててきており、構造形式は「馬木キャンプ」と同じである。

ANGER from the Bottom, a sculpture by Beat Takeshi and Kenji Yanobe, was installed on the site of a well (something that supported people's lives) against a backdrop of Shodoshima's Mt. Doun. In part, it serves as a warning regarding the current relationship between people and nature. This in turn led to the idea of building a shrine for Shinto rituals that would provide a sacred dwelling for rain-making and flood-control deities. *Beat Shrine* is based on the structure of Ise Shrine and Yayoi Period architecture, which apparently inspired Ise Shrine, the building consists of a *hirairi* (side entrance running parallel to the roof ridge), posts driven directly into the ground, posts which directly support the ridge, and a gabled roof with a rectangular gradient. The form is the same as that of *Umaki Camp*.

「ANGER from the Bottom」は最大約6.5mまで伸びる可動式である。そのため「美井戸神社」のコンクリート基礎をシリンダーとすることで、社自体が6,950mmから8,700mmまで、12台の手動油圧ジャッキによって上下伸縮が可能になっている。動く建築は御神輿のような祝祭性をもち、地域の行事と連動する開かれた状況の創出を意図している。

ANGER from the Bottom is a moveable work that can be extended to a maximum of approximately 6.5 meters. As a result, cylinders were installed in the concrete foundation of *Beat Shrine*, making it possible to raise and lower, and expand and contract the shine from between 6,950 mm to 8,700 mm using 12 manual hydraulic jacks. Imbued with a festive quality like a portable shrine, the movable building was intended to create a situation in which local ceremonies can be held.

Beat Shrine   dot architects

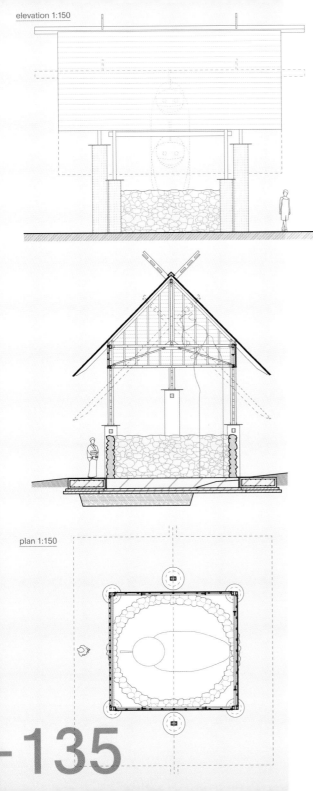

elevation 1:150

plan 1:150

any advanced technology, and to create relationships with a variety of people without a background in construction on the building site. At the same time, by proposing a variety of soft elements such as animals, food, a radio station, movies, and an archive to mediate links between people, and people and the town, new discoveries and ideas emerged out of our cooperative work with the local residents. Though the buildings were made as display works for the Setouchi Triennale in 2013, they continue to function as small social laboratories for welfare, education, and gatherings, and have been maintained in cooperation with local residents and the government.

Beat Shrine was created to protect *ANGER from the Bottom*, a sculpture made by Beat Takeshi and Kenji Yanobe, from the elements, and to serve as a symbol, encouraging people to consider the importance of the local climate and natural environment. First, the Beat Shrine Production Association, consisting of the head of the Shodoshima Residents' Group, members of the business community, and local residents, was launched. Then the association began working to build the shrine using donations from the community. Since the shrine was built, it has been operated and maintained by the Beat Shrine Protection Association and has attracted many people from outside the island.

Today, rather than attempting to distribute objects and information from the center to the periphery, we have entered an era in which direct connections are being made between peripheral areas and communities. While placing special value on the inevitable *en*, one of architecture's roles is to remain open and accept the new accidental *en*.

第15回ヴェネチア・ビエンナーレ国際建築展 日本館

Japan Pavilion
15th International Architecture Exhibition
La Biennale di Venezia 2016

teco

teco

展示デザイン

Venue Design

VENEZIA | 2016

136-

「縁」というテーマで召喚された12作品は、一定敷地において技術や知恵を統合するという建築の性格を踏まえながら、いずれもその領域を拡張し、周縁の地域や人びと、経済、文化や歴史へと触手を伸ばし、関係性を新しく構築する実践である。日本館の展示においては、建築の骨格である壁柱が本展示の3つのテーマ「人の縁」「モノの縁」「地域の縁」の軸を成し、そこから梁空間が広がるかのごとく、12作品が壁柱周縁へと配される。個々の作品により提示される「縁」に加え、作品が互いにその輪郭を重ね、関係付けられることで新たな「縁」が生まれる。一方、日本館の魅力のひとつでもある外構を含めたピロティ空間では、高低差を生かしたアプローチ、種々の樹木や植栽、卍配置の壁柱などによる既存の関係を読み解き、新たに移ろう光や緑の情景を映し出すスクリーンと、人びとの居場所となるしつらえを挿入することで、訪れる人びとのふるまいを紡ぐ「縁」を体感する場とした。

Based on the architectural aspect of fusing technique and knowledge on a specific site, the 12 works, which share the common theme of *en*, expand the space, reaching out toward surrounding areas and people, economies, culture, and history, and functioning as a practical means of building new relationships. In this exhibition in the Japan Pavilion, the wall pillars, the framework of the building, serve as axes for the three main themes: the *en* of people, the *en* of things, and the *en* of locality. Extending out like beams, the 12 works are arranged around these pillars.
In addition to the *en* displayed in each individual work, the contours of the works overlap, creating new *en* by connecting with each other. At the same time, in the piloti space that encompasses the exterior, one of the pavilion's most attractive features, the seats and screens, which display changing scenes of natural light and greenery, are carefully positioned according to an interpretation of the existing relationship between the approach, which makes the most of the natural terrain, various kinds of trees, and the fylfot form of the wall pillars. The space functions as a venue to connect people's behaviors and allow them to experience *en*.

en: art of nexus

ヴェネチア・ビエンナーレ日本館図面
(「吉阪隆正+U研究室」作成／
文化庁国立近現代建築資料館蔵)に
今回の展示計画を加筆(138-141頁)。

The original floor plan for the Japan Pavilion, Venice Biennale (created by YOSIZAKA Takamasa + Atelier U, National Archives of Modern Architecture, Agency for Cultural Affairs, Government of Japan) was revised for this exhibition (pp.138-141).

© National Archives of Modern Architecture, Agency for Cultural Affairs, Government of Japan + teco (pp.138-141).

Padiglione Giappone Biennale Architettura 2016

The *en* of People
1. House for Seven People
   Mio Tsuneyama / mnm
2. Yokohama Apartments
   Osamu Nishida +
   Erika Nakagawa
3. LT Josai
   Naruse Inokuma Architects
4. Apartments with a Small Restaurant
   Naka Architects' Studio

The *en* of Things
5. Guest House in Takaoka
   Nousaku Architects
6. House at Komazawa Park
   Mizuki Imamura +
   Isao Shinohara / miCo.
7. 15A House
   Levi Architecture
8. Boundary Window
   Shingo Masuda +
   Katsuhisa Otsubo Architects
9. The Floor of Atsumi, etc.
   403 architecture [dajiba]
10. House in Chofu
    Koji Aoki Architects

The *en* of Locality
11. Projects in Kamiyama
    BUS
12. Umaki Camp
    Beat Shrine
    dot architects

plan 1:400

first floor

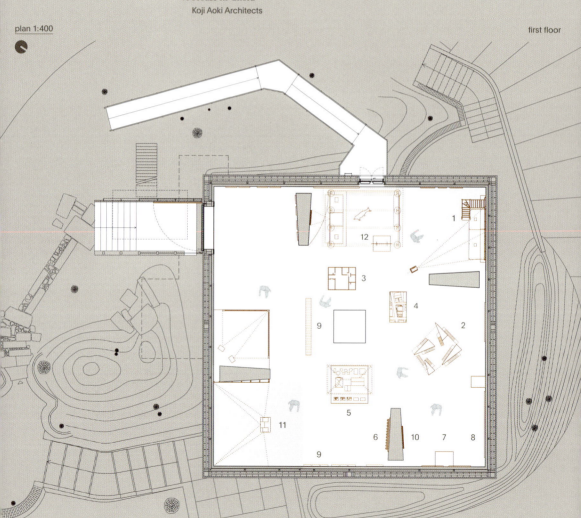

Venue Design | teco

142-

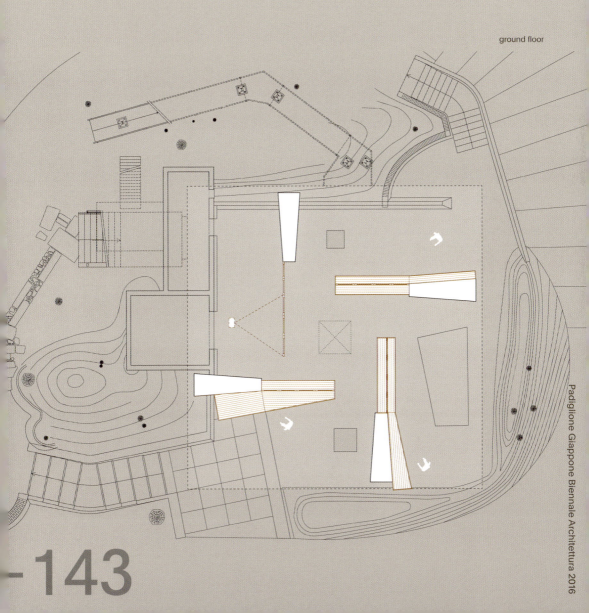
ground floor

144-

Discussion
Profile
Credits
—

論考
プロフィール
クレジット

新自由主義へのミクロな抵抗

佐藤嘉幸

- 経済における新自由主義の導入は、1980年代以来、日本社会のあり方を大きく変化させてきたが、新自由主義が日本社会に浸透するに従って、それに対するミクロな抵抗とも呼び得る実践がさまざまな分野で現れつつある。今回のビエンナーレの日本館企画「en［縁］」にも、そのような実践と解釈できる要素を見出すことができる。

- 新自由主義は、1980年代から各国の政治に適用され、その経済政策を牽引してきた。その中にはむろん、日本も含まれる。日本において、新自由主義は1980年代に中曽根政権(1982-1987年)において導入され、国営企業(国鉄、電電公社、専売公社)の民営化を中心に、公的セクターの民営化を推進した。新自由主義は2000年代には小泉政権(2001-2006年)において集中的に展開され、社会全体へと拡大された。小泉政権はその民営化政策(郵政民営化、国立大学の独立法人化など)によって国家公務員を半減させ、同時に、労働分野の規制緩和によって非正規労働者を雇用全体の3分の1にまでに増加させ、貧困層の大幅な増加を生み出した。このように新自由主義は、第1に、貧富の格差を拡大し、富裕層をさらに富ませ、貧困層をさらに窮乏化させる。そしてそれは、第2に、社会全体を競争原理によって組織する。

- 第1点から述べていこう。新自由主義とは市場主義を原理とした統治技法であり、すべてを市場に委ね、貧富の格差を増大させる。

- 第二次世界大戦後の経済を支配してきたのは、ケインズ主義的な福祉国家政策であった。ケインズ主義は、市場は不合理性を含む、という前提に立って、市場の歪みを修正するような福祉国家政策を採用していた。それは、累進課税制度を通じた所得の再配分、社会保障によるリスクの社会化(個々人がもつ失業、病気、事故などのリスクを社会全体で支えること)を手段として、貧富の格差とそれに由来する社会的不平等を是正しようとした。なぜなら、資本主義経済においてすべてを市場に委ねれば、貧富の格差が累進的に拡大し、社会は二極化、不安定化していくからである。

- それに対して新自由主義は、その市場主義という原理ゆえに、ケインズ主義が採用してきた福祉国家政策を放棄あるいは縮減する(「大きな政府」
から「小さな政府」への移行)。所得の再分配は、累進課税の
縮小(高所得者の減税)、間接税の導入(低所得者の増税)、

A Micro-resistance to Neoliberalism

Yoshiyuki Sato

- The introduction of economic neoliberalism has led to drastic changes in Japanese society since the 1980s, but the permeation of such policies has also inspired practices that might be seen as a "micro-resistance" in a wide range of fields. The *en* exhibition, set to be held in the Japan Pavilion at this year's Venice Biennale, also contains elements that can be seen as examples of such practices.

- In the '80s, neoliberalism was adopted by various governments around the world as a means of driving economic policy. Japan was of course one of these countries. Here, neoliberalism was first introduced by the Nakasone administration (1982-1987), and used to promote the privatization of the public sector, in particular state-owned enterprises such as Japanese National Railways, Nippon Telegraph and Telephone Public Corporation, and Japan Tobacco and Salt Public Corporation. In the '00s, these policies was developed more extensively by the Koizumi administration (2001-2006), and expanded to include society as a whole. Koizumi's privatization policy, which included privatizing the postal system and turning national universities into independent corporations, halved the number of national government employees. In addition, it reclassified one third of the labor force as non-regular workers through the deregulation of labor laws, leading to a substantial increase in poverty. Above all, neoliberalism increases the wealth disparity, making the rich richer, and the poor poorer. This, in turn, creates an overall social structure that is based on the principles of competition.

- Let us take a closer look at the first point. Neoliberalism is a governmental technique based on a market economy, which, by entrusting everything to the market, widens the gap between rich and poor.

- The post-World War II economy was bolstered by a Keynesian welfare-state policy. Keynesian economics is based on the premise that the market contains an element of irrationality, and that the adoption of welfare-state policies will help correct these distortions. Then, by redistributing income through a progressive taxation system and socializing risk through a social security system (i.e., using society as a whole to support individual risks such as unemployment, illness, and accident), an effort is made to redress the wealth disparity and the social inequality that stems from it. This is because simply leaving everything to the market in a capitalist economy will lead to a progressively widening gap between rich and poor, and lead to polariza-

法人税の大幅減税によって、ほぼ理念としては無化されつつある。また新自由主義は、規制緩和によって労働市場を「フレキシブル化」して——すなわち、不況時に労働者を解雇しやすくし、賃金を下げやすくして——、非正規雇用、期限付き雇用を導入し、労働者とその労働環境を不安定化している。それらの経済政策の実現によって、貧富の差は拡大し、社会は二極化、不安定化しつつある。実際、日本において、長期的な不況が始まった1997年には、「ワーキング・プア」と呼ばれる年収200万円以下の低賃金層は全体の17.9％であったのに対して、リーマン・ショックによって不況が極大化した2009年には24.5％にまで増大している。市場に介入して市場の歪みを修正する、という福祉国家政策を放棄することで、新自由主義的統治は、貧富の格差を増大させ続け、資本主義は19世紀のような苛烈な搾取、社会の二極化へと逆戻りしているのである。オキュパイ運動において叫ばれた「私たちは99％だ」(つまり、人口の1％程度が莫大な富を独占し、その富を累進的に増大させている)というスローガンは、まさしくこのような、貧富の格差を累進的に増大させ続ける新自由主義的統治を批判したものであった。

- 第2に、新自由主義は社会全体を競争原理によって組織しようとする。新自由主義は、競争が存在しない場所に競争を設計し、すべての人びとを競争原理によって統治しようとする。それは単に国営企業を民営化するだけではなく、労働環境に成果別賃金のような競争原理を導入し、競争に勝てない経済主体を積極的に排除し、利益の追求がふさわしくないような教育(国民教育、大学)や文化(美術館)のようなセクターにまで競争原理を強要して、社会全体を競争原理で満たそうとしている。そして、そうした新自由主義政策に適応すべく、個々の主体は、競争原理を内面化した「競争的主体」へと自らを変化させ、競争によって分断され、互いに個人化していくのである。

- 2011年3月の東日本大震災と福島第一原発事故は、このような新自由主義化が進展する日本社会に、ふたつの正反対の帰結をもたらした。一方で、震災と原発事故後の日本社会では、「ショック・ドクトリン」(ナオミ・クライン)、すなわち惨事便乗型資本主義が展開されている。震災と原発事故はさまざまな意味で既存の共同体とその社会基盤を破壊したが、その「復興＝再建」の過程では、被災地の企業ではなく中央の大企業が利潤の大部分を収奪している。このように、震災と原発事故は、その「復興＝再建」の過程において、新自由主義をさらに深化させる帰結を生んでいるのである。

tion and destabilization in society.

— In contrast, due to a belief in the market economy, neoliberalism sets out to abandon or limit Keynesian welfare-state policies (in order to facilitate a shift from "big" to "small" government). Reducing progressive taxation (decreasing taxes for high-income earners), introducing indirect taxation (increasing taxes for low-income earners), and greatly lowering the corporate tax, essentially nullifies the idea of redistributing wealth. Neoliberalism also strives to "flexibilize" the labor market through deregulation (in other words, make it easier to lay off workers and lower wages during a recession), introduce non-regular and fixed-term employment, and "precarize" workers and the labor environment. The implementation of these economic policies has led to an increase in the wealth disparity, and greater social polarization and destabilization. In fact, in 1997, the beginning of Japan's long-term recession, low-income households (the so-called "working poor," with annual incomes of less than 2 million yen) accounted for 17.9 percent of the labor force. But in 2009, when the recession was exacerbated by the global financial crisis, this number rose to 24.5 percent. By abandoning the state-welfare policy of correcting distortion through market intervention, neoliberal governmentality has increased the wealth disparity, and reverted to a type of capitalism that recalls the harsh exploitation and social polarization of the 19th century. The protest slogan of the Occupy movement, "We are the 99%" (i.e., approximately one percent of the population possesses a vast amount of wealth and that wealth is progressively increasing), is nothing less than a criticism of these neoliberal governmentality that continues to widen the gap between rich and poor.

— Second, neoliberalism sets out to organize society according to the principle of competition. This policy creates competition in places where it did not previously exist, and attempts to govern all of the people using competitive principles. This does not simply mean privatizing state-owned enterprises, but also includes introducing principles such as a performance-based wage system, actively eliminating economic agents that are not competitive, and forcing sectors such as education (national education and universities) and culture (museums), which are not concerned with the pursuit of profit, to adopt a competitive approach in order to meet all the needs of society as a whole through competition. Then each individual, which is expected to adapt to neoliberal policies, will interiorize the competitive principle and transform itself into a competitive subject. Through competition, they will in turn be divided and individuated from each other.

The Great East Japan Earthquake and subsequent accident at the Fukushima Daiichi Nuclear Power Plant in March 2011 produced two completely

- 他方で、震災と原発事故後には、被災地でのボランティア活動や新たな共同性の構築を通じて、新自由主義へのミクロな抵抗が形成されつつある。ボランティア活動で被災地に入った若者たちは、その後、被災地で新たな共同性を組織する、政治的意識に目覚めて抵抗運動を組織する、といった新たな実践を開始している。とりわけ後者の傾向は、2011年3月以後、数多くの脱原発デモとして、そして2015年春以後、集団的自衛権行使を容認する安保法制への反対デモとして顕在化している。

- 最後に、今回の「en［縁］」に集められた建築において、こうしたミクロな抵抗の実践として解釈できる要素とは何だろうか。3点だけ指摘しておきたい。

- 第1に、シェアによる「共生」が重視されている。これは、新自由主義の競争原理が生み出す個々人の分断に対する、ひとつのオルタナティヴとして解釈することができる。

- 第2に、リサイクル、リユースが重視されている。これは、私たちが福島原発事故によって身をもって知った「環境」への配慮の重要性に対する、建築家の側からの応答として解釈することができる。

- 第3に、過疎化した地方でのさまざまな建築実践が、新たな人的交流を組織し、新たな文化実践を創造する契機をもたらしている。これは、地方で進展しつつある新自由主義的な「選択と集中」政策へのミクロな抵抗を形成していると解釈することもできるだろう。

- 私たちはこれら3つの傾向に、重厚長大な建築とは異なった、新自由主義へのオルタナティヴとしての新たな建築の潮流を見出すことができるのである。

contradictory effects in Japan's increasing neoliberal society. The first was a "shock doctrine" (Naomi Klein) – a kind of "disaster capitalism." While these calamities destroyed existing communities and the social foundation in many different ways, in the reconstruction process, the majority of the profits were seized by large corporations based in the center instead of companies based in the stricken area. In this sense, the disaster produced consequences that strengthened neoliberalism.

— At the same time, the earthquake and nuclear accident inspired a micro-resistance to neoliberalism through volunteer activities and the creation of new communities in the stricken area. Young volunteers adopted a new practical approach by organizing communities in the disaster area, and after attaining a new political awareness, launched a resistance movement. The latter trend was most apparent in the countless anti-nuclear demonstrations that have occurred since March 2011, and the protests against national security legislation that recognizes the right of collective self-defense that have been held since the spring of 2015.

— In closing, I would like to consider elements in the collection of architectural works in the *en* exhibition that might be seen as acts of micro-resistance by citing just three examples.

— First, there is a strong emphasis on living together as exemplified by the shared aspect of many of the works. This can be viewed as an alternative to the trend toward dividing individuals that emerged from neoliberalism's competitive principles.

— Second, there is a strong emphasis on recycling and reusing things. This can be viewed as the architects' response to the importance of the environment – something we learned firsthand in the Fukushima nuclear accident.

— Third, various architectural practices in depopulated areas provide an opportunity for new personal exchanges and cultural endeavors. This can be viewed as a micro-resistance to the neoliberal policy of "selection and concentration," which has become increasingly pervasive in regional areas.

— In these three tendencies, we can detect a new architectural current, which unlike massive and heavy architecture, functions as an alternative to neoliberalism.

プロフィール　　　　　　　　　　　　　Profile

01

キュレーター

山名善之 | やまなよしゆき | 01
東京理科大学理工学部建築学科教授
フランス政府公認建築家DPLG、博士(美術史)
専門：建築史・意匠学、アーカイブズ学
ICOMOS、DOCOMOMOのメンバーとして
建築保存（近現代建築）、文化遺産分野で活動。

1966年東京都文京区生まれ。1990年東京理科大学卒業。香山アトリエ／環境造形研究所、パリ・ベルヴィル建築学校DPLG課程（フランス政府給費留学生）、パリ大学パンテオン・ソルボンヌ校博士課程。アンリ・シリニア・アトリエ（パリ・文化庁在外派遣芸術家研修員）、ナント建築大学契約講師等を経て、2002年より東京理科大学勤務。

02

制作委員会

菱川勢一 | ひしかわせいいち | 02
クリエイティブディレクター、映像作家／写真家
DRAWING AND MANUAL ファウンダー、
武蔵野美術大学教授

1969年東京生まれ。レコード会社、家電メーカー宣伝部、海外音楽チャンネル番組制作、ハリウッド映画予告編制作など多岐にわたる経験を持ち、TVCMやミュージックビデオの映像監督、企業ブランディングやWebサイトのアートディレクター、ファッションやイベントなどの舞台監督を歴任。ニューヨークADC賞、ロンドン国際広報賞など国際的な受賞多数。2011年に監督を務めたNTTドコモのCM「森の木琴」がカンヌライオンズにて三冠を受賞。

03

内野正樹 | うちのまさき | 03
エディター

1960年静岡県生まれ。雑誌『建築文化』で、ル・コルビュジエ、ミース・ファン・デル・ローエら巨匠の全冊特集を企画・編集するほか、映画や思想、美術等、他ジャンルと建築との接点を探る特集も手がける。同誌編集長を経て、『DETAIL JAPAN』を創刊。現在、ecrimageを主宰。著書に『一流建築家のデザインと

04

Curator

Yoshiyuki Yamana | 01
Professor, Department of Architecture,
Tokyo University of Science
French-registered Architect (DPLG),
Doctorate in Art History
Specialties: Architectural Design,
Architectural History, and Archival Science
Senior Curator, the National Archive of
Modern Architecture
Visiting Researcher, the National Museum of Western Art
Advisory Board member, DOCOMOMO International
Vice-Chairman, Docomomo Japan
Committee member, ICOMOS Japan

Born in 1966 in Tokyo, Yoshiyuki Yamana graduated from the Department of Architecture at Tokyo University of Science (TUS) in 1990, and worked at Koyama. Receiving a scholarship for foreign students from the French government, he studied at Ecole Nationale Supérieure d'Architecture de Paris-Belleville and obtained a degree in architecture (DPLG). He then obtained a doctoral degree from the Université Paris 1 Panthéon-Sorbonne. After being trained at the Henri Ciriani Atelier, as part of the Agency for Cultural Affairs' overseas training program for artists, he worked as a contract lecturer at the Ecole d'architecture, Nantes, the Archives de France, and the Institut français d'architecture. He began working at the Department of Architecture of TUS in 2002.

Deputy Curators

Seiichi Hishikawa | 02
Creative Director
Filmmaker/Photographer
Founder, DRAWING AND MANUAL
Professor, Musashino Art University

Born in 1969 in Tokyo. Through a wide variety of working career at a record company and PR of an electronics manufacturer; producing overseas music programs and hollywood movie previews, he has directed many TVCM, music videos, corporate sites or web brandings, and fashion events and theatoricals. Gained many international prizes such as NYADC and London International Awards and in 2011, he was triple awarded at Cannes Lions International Festival of Creativity with his directorial webCM for Docomo, "Xylophone."

Masaki Uchino | 03
Editor

Masaki Uchino was
born in 1960 in
Shizuoka Prefecture.
In addition to

その現場』、『表参道を歩いてわかる現代建築』(以上、共著)、『パリ建築散歩』(大和書房、2014)がある。

篠原雅武 | しのはらまさたけ | 04

大阪大学国際公共政策研究科特任准教授

京都大学人文科学研究所非常勤講師、

博士 (人間・環境学)

専門：哲学、思想史、都市空間論

1975年神奈川県生まれ。1999年京都大学総合人間学部卒業。2007年京都大学大学院人間・環境学研究科博士課程修了。2012年より、大阪大学公共政策研究科特任准教授。著書として、『公共空間の政治理論』(人文書院、2007)、『空間のために：遍在化するスラム的世界のなかで』(以文社、2011)、『全‐生活論：転形期の公共空間』(以文社、2012)、『生きられたニュータウン：未来空間の哲学』(青土社、2015)。

出展作家

mnm | **常山未央** | つねやまみお | 05

1983年神奈川県生まれ。2005年東京理科大学工学部第二部建築学科卒業。2005-2006年ブノート・ザパタアーキテクツ(スイス)。2006-2008年スイス政府給費留学生。2008年スイス連邦工科大学ローザンヌ校建築学科修士課程修了。2008-2012年HHFアーキテクツ(スイス)勤務。2012年mnm設立。2013-2015年東京理科大学工学部第二部建築学科補手、2015年より同校助教。2014年より武蔵野美術大学造形学部建築学科非常勤講師。

西田司 | にしだおさむ | 06

1976年神奈川県生まれ。1999年横浜国立大学卒業。建築設計SPEED STUDIO設立・主宰。2002-2007年東京都立大学大学院助手。2004年オンデザインパートナーズ設立。2005-2009年横浜国立大学(Y-GSA)助手。2013-2016年東京大学、東京理科大学非常勤講師。

中川エリカ | なかがわえりか | 07

1983年東京都生まれ。2005年横浜国立大学工学部建設学科建築学コース卒業。2007年東京藝術大学大学院美術

planning and producing whole magazine features on master architects, such as Le Corbusier and Mies van der Rohe, for the magazine Kenchiku Bunka [Architectural culture], he searched for common points of contact between architecture and genres such as film, philosophy, and art. After working as editor of the same magazine, he founded a new publication called DETAIL JAPAN. He is currently the director of ecrimage. His published works include *Ichiryu Kenchikuka no Dezain to Sono Genba* [Designs and sites of top architects], and *Omotesando wo Aruite Wakaru Gendai Kenchiku* [Understanding contemporary architecture by walking through Omotesando] (both of which he co-wrote), and *Pari Kenchiku Sanpo* [A walking guide to Paris architecture].

Masatake Shinohara | 04
Specially Appointed Associate Professor,
Osaka University
Part-time Lecturer, Kyoto University
Doctorate in Human and Environmental Studies
Specialties: Philosophy, History of Thought,
Urban Space Theory

Masatake Shinohara was born in 1975 in Kanagawa Prefecture. After graduating from the Faculty of Integrated Human Studies, Kyoto University, he went on studying at the Graduate School of Human and Environment Studies of the same university for a doctoral program. He currently serves as a specially appointed associate professor at Osaka School of International Public Policy, Osaka University. His publications include *Kokyo Kukan no Seiji Riron* [Political theory of public space] (Jimbun Shoin, 2007), *Kukan no tame ni: Henzaika suru Suramuteki Shakai no Nakade* [For spaces: In omnipresent slum-like world] (Ibunsha, 2011), *Zen-Seikatsuron: Tenkeiki no Kokyo Kukan* [An essay on the conception of whole-life: public space in transformation] (Ibunsha, 2012), and *Ikirareta Nyu Taun: Mirai Kukan no Tetsugaku* [On the lived New Town: philosophy of future space] (Seidosha, 2015).

Exhibitors

mnm | Mio Tsuneyama | 05

Born in in 1983 Kanagawa Prefecture, Mio Tsuneyama graduated from Tokyo University of Science (TUS) in 2005. She did an internship at Bonhôte Zapata Architectes Genève, Switzerland from 2005 to 2006. From 2006 to 2008, she was given Swiss International Student Bourse and completed a graduate course in architecture at École Polytechnique Fédéral de Lausanne, Switzerland in 2008. After working at HHF Architects Basel, Switzerland, she established Studio mnm in 2012. She worked as an assistant at TUS from 2013 and became an assistant professor in 2015. She also started teaching at Musashino Art University as a part-time lecturer in 2014.

Osamu Nishida | 06

Osamu Nishida was born in 1976 in Kanagawa Prefecture. He graduated from Yokohama National University in 1999. In 2002, he established the architecture firm

05

06

07

08

研究科修了。2007-2014年オンデザイン勤務。2014年中川エリカ建築設計事務所設立。2012年横浜国立大学非常勤講師。2014-2016年横浜国立大学大学院(Y-GSA)設計助手。2016年より東京藝術大学非常勤講師。

成瀬・猪熊建築設計事務所 | 猪熊純 | いのくまじゅん | 08
1977年神奈川県生まれ。2004年東京大学大学院修士課程修了。2006年まで千葉学建築計画事務所勤務。2007年成瀬・猪熊建築設計事務所共同設立。2008年から首都大学東京助教。

09

成瀬・猪熊建築設計事務所 | 成瀬友梨 | なるせゆり | 09
1979年愛知県生まれ。2007年東京大学大学院博士課程単位取得退学。2007年成瀬・猪熊建築設計事務所共同設立。2009年東京大学特任助教。2010年より同助教。

仲建築設計スタジオ | 仲俊治 | なかとしはる | 10
1976年京都府生まれ。1999年東京大学工学部建築学科卒業。2001年東京大学大学院工学系研究科建築学専攻修了。2001-2008年株式会社山本理顕設計工場勤務。2009年株式会社仲建築設計スタジオ設立。2009-2011年横浜国立大学大学院Y-GSA設計助手。2011-2014年東京都市大学非常勤講師、2015年東京大学非常勤講師。現在、横浜国立大学、明治大学、関東学院大学にて非常勤講師。

10

11

仲建築設計スタジオ | 宇野悠里 | うのゆうり | 11
1976年東京都生まれ。1999年東京大学工学部建築学科卒業。2001年東京大学大学院工学系研究科建築学専攻修了。2001-2013年株式会社日本設計勤務。2013年より株式会社 仲建築設計スタジオ共同主宰。

12

能作アーキテクツ | 能作文徳 | のうさくふみのり | 12
1982年富山県生まれ。2005年東京工業大学建築学科卒業。2007年東京工業大学大学院建築学専攻修士課程修了。2008年 Njiric+Arhitekti 勤務。2010年東京工業大学補佐員。2010年能作文徳建築設計事務所設立。2012年東京工業大学大学院建築学専攻博士課程修了。2012年より東京工業大学大学院建築学専攻助教。

13

Speed Studio. From 2002 to 2007 he worked as a graduate assistant at Tokyo Metropolitan University Graduate School, and he established ondesign in 2004. He worked as an assistant at Yokohama Graduate School of Architecture (Y-GSA) from 2005 to 2009 and works as a part-time lecturer at the University of Tokyo and Tokyo University of Science from 2013 to 2016.

Erika Nakagawa | 07
Erika Nakagawa was born in 1983 in Tokyo. She graduated from Yokohama National University in 2005 and obtained her master's degree from Graduate School of Fine Arts, Tokyo University of the Arts in 2007. She worked at ondesign between 2007 and 2014. In 2014, she established erika nakagawa office. She worked as part-time lecturer at Yokohama National University in 2012, and currently works as a design assistant at Y-GSA from 2014 to 2016. She starts teaching at Tokyo University of the Arts as a part-time lecturer in 2016.

Naruse Inokuma Architects | Jun Inokuma | 08
Born in 1977 in Kanagawa Prefecture, Jun Inokuma earned a master's degree in architecture from the University of Tokyo in 2004. He worked at Chiba Manabu Architects until 2006, and established Naruse Inokuma Architects with Yuri Naruse in 2007. He became an assistant professor at Tokyo Metropolitan University in 2008.

Naruse Inokuma Architects | Yuri Naruse | 09
Yuri Naruse was born in 1979 in Aichi Prefecture. In 2007, she completed her doctoral program in architecture at the University of Tokyo and established Naruse Inokuma Architects with Jun Inokuma. She became a project research associate at the graduate school of the University of Tokyo in 2009 and a research associate at the same school in 2010.

Naka Architects' Studio | Toshiharu Naka | 10
Toshiharu Naka was born in 1976 in Kyoto Prefecture. After graduating from the Department of Architecture at the University of Tokyo in 1999, he earned a master's degree in architecture from the University of Tokyo in 2001. He worked at Riken Yamamoto & Field Shop from 2001 to 2008, and established Naka Architects' Studio in 2009. Then he worked as a design assistant at Y-GSA from 2009 to 2011. He also works as a part-time lecturer at Yokohama National University, Meiji University and Kanto Gakuin University.

Naka Architects' Studio | Yuri Uno | 11
Yuri Uno was born in 1976 in Tokyo. After graduating from the Department of Architecture at the University of Tokyo in 1999, she earned a master's degree in architecture from
the University of
Tokyo in 2001. She
worked at Nihon
Sekkei from 2001
to 2013 and joined

能作アーキテクツ | 能作淳平 | のうさくじゅんぺい | 13
1983年富山県生まれ。2006年武蔵工業大学卒業。2006-2010年長谷川豪建築設計事務所勤務。2010年能作淳平建築設計事務所設立。

miCo. | 今村水紀 | いまむらみずき | 14
1975年神奈川県生まれ。1999年明治大学理工学部建築学科卒業。2001-2008年妹島和世建築設計事務所勤務。2008年miCo.設立。現在女子美術大学、日本工業大学、明治大学、東京理科大学、日本大学非常勤講師。

miCo. | 篠原勲 | しのはらいさお | 15
1977年愛知県生まれ。2003年慶應義塾大学大学院政策・メディア研究科修士課程修了。2003-2013年SANAA勤務。2008年miCo.設立。現在女子美術大学、東京理科大学、昭和女子大学非常勤講師。

レビ設計室 | 中川純 | なかがわじゅん | 16
1976年神奈川県生まれ。2003年早稲田大学理工学部建築学科卒業。2003-2006年難波和彦・界工作舎勤務。2006年レビ設計室設立。2013年早稲田大学理工学研究所研究員。2014年より早稲田大学大学院田辺新一研究室在籍。

増田信吾+大坪克亘 | 増田信吾 | ますだしんご | 17
1982年東京都生まれ。2007年武蔵野美術大学卒業。2007年増田信吾+大坪克亘共同主宰。2010年より武蔵野美術大学非常勤講師、2015年よりコーネル大学客員教授。

増田信吾+大坪克亘 | 大坪克亘 | おおつぼかつひさ | 18
1983年埼玉県生まれ。2007年東京藝術大学卒業。2007年増田信吾+大坪克亘共同主宰。

青木弘司建築設計事務所 | 青木弘司 | あおきこうじ | 19
1976年北海道生まれ。2001年北海学園大学工学部建築学科卒業。2003年室蘭工業大学大学院修了。2003-2011年藤本壮介建築設計事務所勤務。2011年青木弘司建築設計事務所設立。2013-2015年東

Naka Architects' Studio as a partner in 2013.

Nousaku Architects | Fuminori Nousaku | 12
Born in 1982 in Toyama Prefecture, Fuminori Nousaku graduated from the Department of Architecture and Building Engineering at the Tokyo Institute of Technology in 2005. He then earned a master's degree from the same institute in 2007. After working at Njiric+Arhitekti in 2008, he became a research associate at the Tokyo Institute of Technology in 2010. He established Fuminori Nousaku Architects in 2010 and obtained a doctorate in architecture from the Tokyo Institute of Technology in 2012. In the same year, he became an assistant professor at the same institute.

Nousaku Architects | Junpei Nousaku | 13
Junpei Nousaku was born in 1983 in Toyama Prefecture. He graduated from the Department of Architecture at the Musashi Institute of Technology (now Tokyo City University) in 2006. After working at Go Hasegawa & Associates from 2006 to 2010, he established Junpei Nousaku Architects in 2010.

miCo. | Mizuki Imamura | 14
Mizuki Imamura was born in 1975 in Kanagawa Prefecture and graduated from the Department of Architecture at Meiji University in 1999. After working at SANAA from 2001 to 2008, she established miCo. in 2008. She currently works as a part-time lecturer at Joshibi University of Art and Design, Nippon Institute of Technology, Meiji University, TUS, and Nihon University.

miCo. | Isao Shinohara | 15
Isao Shinohara was born in 1977 in Aichi Prefecture. He obtained his master's degree from the Graduate School of Media and Governance of Keio University in 2003. While working at SANAA from 2003 to 2013, he established miCo. in 2008. He currently works as a part-time lecturer at Joshibi University of Art and Design, TUS, and Showa Women's University.

Levi Architecture | Jun Nakagawa | 16
Jun Nakagawa was born in 1976 in Kanagawa Prefecture. After graduating from the Department of Architecture at Waseda University in 2003, he worked at the Kazuhiko Namba + Kai Workshop until 2006. He established Levi Architecture in 2006 and became a researcher at Research Institute for Science and Engineering Waseda University in 2013. In the following year, he joined the Shin-ichi Tanabe Laboratory at Waseda University. He currently works as a part-time lecturer at the University of Tokyo and Tokyo Metropolitan University.

Shingo Masuda+Katsuhisa Otsubo Architects Shingo Masuda | 17
Shingo Masuda was born in 1982 in Tokyo and graduated from Musashino Art University in 2007. He established Shingo Masuda+Katsuhisa Otsubo Architects with Katsuhisa Otsubo in 2007. He started working as a part-time lecturer at Musashino Art University in 2010. He

14

15

16

17

18

19

京理科大学非常勤講師。現在、武蔵野美術大学、東京造形大学、東京大学非常勤講師。

403architecture [dajiba] | 彌田徹 | やだとおる | 20
1985年大分県生まれ。2008年横浜国立大学建設学科建築学コース卒業。2011年筑波大学大学院芸術専攻貝島研究室修了。2011年403architecture [dajiba]設立。現在、筑波大学非常勤講師。

403architecture [dajiba] | 辻琢磨 | つじたくま | 21
1986年静岡県生まれ。2008年横浜国立大学建設学科建築学コース卒業。2010年横浜国立大学大学院建築都市スクールY-GSA修了。2010年Urban Nouveau*勤務。2011年メディアプロジェクト・アンテナ企画運営。2011年403architecture [dajiba]設立。現在、滋賀県立大学、大阪市立大学非常勤講師。

403architecture [dajiba]
橋本健史 | はしもとたけし | 22
1984年兵庫県生まれ。2005年国立明石工業高等専門学校建築学科卒業。2008年横浜国立大学建設学科建築学コース卒業。2010年横浜国立大学大学院建築都市スクールY-GSA修了。2011年403architecture [dajiba]設立。現在、名城大学、筑波大学非常勤講師。

BUS | 伊藤暁 | いとうさとる | 23
1976年東京都生まれ。2000年横浜国立大学工学部建設学科卒業。2002年横浜国立大学大学院工学研究科修士課程修了。2002-2006年aat+ヨコミゾマコト建築設計事務所勤務。2007年伊藤暁建築設計事務所設立。

BUS | 坂東幸輔 | ばんどうこうすけ | 24
1979年徳島県生まれ。2002年東京藝術大学美術学部建築科卒業。2002-2004年スキーマ建築計画勤務。2008年ハーバード大学大学院デザインスクール修了。2009年ティーハウス建築設計事務所勤務。2010年坂東幸輔建築設計事務所設立。2010年BUS設立。2010-2013年東京藝術大学美術学部建築科教育研究助手。2013年aat+ヨコミゾマコト建築設計事務所勤務。2015年より京都市立芸術大学講師。

also serves as a visiting critic at Cornell University in 2015.

Shingo Masuda + Katsuhisa Otsubo Architects
Katsuhisa Otsubo | 18
Born in 1983 in Saitama Prefecture, Katsuhisa Otsubo graduated from Tokyo University of the Arts in 2007. He established Shingo Masuda + Katsuhisa Otsubo Architects with Shingo Masuda in 2007.

Koji Aoki Architects | **Koji Aoki** | 19
Koi Aoki was born in 1976 in Hokkaido. After graduating from the Department of Architecture at Hokkai Gakuen University in 2001, he earned a master's degree in architecture from Muroran Institute of Technology in 2003. He worked at Sou Fujimoto Architects from 2003 to 2011, and established Koji Aoki Architects in 2011. He worked as a part-time lecturer at Tokyo University of Science from 2013 to 2015. He also works as a part-time lecturer at Musashino Art University, Tokyo Zokei University and The University of Tokyo.

403architecture [dajiba] | **Toru Yada** | 20
Toru Yada was born in 1985 in Oita Prefecture. After graduating from the Department of Architecture and Building Science at Yokohama National University in 2008, he obtained a master's degree from momoyo kaijima lab. of University of Tsukuba in 2011. He established 403architecture [dajiba] in 2011. He currently works as a part¬time lecturer at University of Tsukuba.

403architecture [dajiba] | **Takuma Tsuji** | 21
Takuma Tsuji was born in 1986 in Shizuoka Prefecture. After graduating from the Department of Architecture and Building Science at Yokohama National University in 2008, he obtained a master's degree from Yokohama Graduate School of Architecture in 2010. He then worked at Urban Nouveau* in 2010. In 2011, he started the Untenor media project and established 403architecture [dajiba]. He currently works as a part-time lecturer at Osaka City University and University of Shiga Prefecture.

403architecture [dajiba] | **Takeshi Hashimoto** | 22
Born in 1984 in Hyogo Prefecture, Takeshi Hashimoto graduated from the architecture department at National Institute of Technology, Akashi College in 2005. After graduated from t the Department of Architecture and Building Science at Yokohama National University in 2008, he obtained a master's degree from Yokohama Graduate School of Architecture in 2010. In 2011, he established 403architecture [dajiba]. He currently works as a part-time lecturer at Meijo University and University of Tsukuba.

BUS | **Satoru Ito** | 23
Satoru Ito was born in 1976 in Tokyo. After graduating from the Department of Engineering at Yokohama

BUS | 須磨一清 | すまいっせい | 25

1976年東京都生まれ。1999年慶應義塾大学環境情報学部卒業。2002年コロンビア大学建築修士科卒業。2004-2007年 ROCKWELL GROUP 勤務。2007-2010年 VOORSANGER ARCHTECHTS 勤務。2011年須磨設計設立。

ドットアーキテクツ | 家成俊勝 | いえなりとしかつ | 26

1974年兵庫県生まれ。1998年関西大学法学部法律学科卒業。2000年大阪工業技術専門学校夜間部卒業。2004年ドットアーキテクツ共同主宰。現在京都造形芸術大学特任准教授、大阪工業技術専門学校非常勤講師。

ドットアーキテクツ | 赤代武志 | しゃくしろたけし | 27

1974年兵庫県生まれ。1997年神戸芸術工科大学芸術工学部環境デザイン学科卒業。北村陸夫+ズーム計画工房、宮本佳明建築設計事務所を経て、2004年ドットアーキテクツ共同主宰。現在大阪工業技術専門学校特任教員、神戸芸術工科大学非常勤講師。

ドットアーキテクツ | 土井亘 | どいわたる | 28

1987年神奈川県生まれ。2013年慶應義塾大学政策・メディア研究科修士課程修了。studio mumbai architectsを経て、2014年よりドットアーキテクツに参画。

National University in 2000, he earned his master's degree in 2002. He worked at aat+Makoto Yokomizo Architects from 2002 to 2006 and then established Satoru Ito Architects and Associates in 2007.

BUS | Kosuke Bando | 24

Kosuke Bando was born in 1979 in Tokushima Prefecture. After graduating from the Department of Architecture at Tokyo University of the Arts in 2002, he worked at Schemata Architecture until 2004. In 2008, he obtained his master's degree from Harvard University Graduate School of Design. Then he worked at Architects Teehouse in 2009 and established Kosuke Bando Architects in 2010. In 2010, he also established BUS. He worked as a teaching assistant at Tokyo University of the Arts from 2010 to 2013, and at aat+Makoto Yokomizo Architects in 2013. He currently works at Kyoto City University of Arts as a lecturer.

BUS | Issei Suma | 25

Issei Suma was born in 1976 in Tokyo. After graduating from the Faculty of Environment and Information Studies at Keio University in 1999, he obtained his master's degree from Columbia University in 2002. He worked at the Rockwell Group from 2004 to 2007 and at Voorsanger Architects from 2007 to 2010. He established SUMA in 2011.

dot architects | Toshikatsu Ienari | 26

Toshikatsu Ienari was born in 1974 in Hyogo Prefecture. He graduated from the Faculty of Law at Kansai University in 1998 and from the Osaka College of Technology in 2000. In 2004, he established dot architects. He currently works as an associate professor at Kyoto University of Art and Design, and a part-time lecturer at Osaka College of Technology

dot architects | Takeshi Shakushiro | 27

Born in 1974 in Hyogo Prefecture, Takeshi Shakushiro graduated from the Department of Environmental Design at Kobe Design University in 1997. He worked at Rikuo Kitamura + Zoom Atelier, and Katsuhiro Miyamoto & Associates before establishing dot architects in 2004. He currently works as a specially appointed lecturer at Osaka College of Technology and part-time lecturer at Kobe Design University.

dot architects | Wataru Doi | 28

Wataru Doi was born in 1987 in Kanagawa Prefecture and earned a master's degree from the Graduate School of Media and Governance of Keio University in 2013. After working at Studio Mumbai Architects, he Joined dot architects in 2014.

26

27

28

映像

菱川勢一 | ひしかわせいいち | 02
[制作委員会の項を参照]

会場デザイン

29

teco | 金野千恵 | こんのちえ | 29
1981年神奈川県生まれ。2005年東京工業大学工学部建築学科卒業。同大学院在学中、スイス連邦工科大学奨学生。2011年東京工業大学大学院博士課程修了、博士(工学)取得。2011-2012年神戸芸術工科大学大学院助手、KONNO設立。2013年より日本工業大学助教。2015年teco設立。

30

teco | アリソン理恵 | ありそんりえ | 30
1982年宮崎県生まれ。2005年東京工業大学工学部建築学科卒業。2011年東京工業大学大学院博士課程単位取得退学。2011-14年ルートエー勤務。2014-15年アトリエ・アンド・アイ坂本一成研究室勤務。2015年teco設立。

論考

31

佐藤嘉幸 | さとうよしゆき | 31
1971年京都府生まれ。京都大学大学院経済学研究科博士課程修了後、パリ第10大学にて博士号(哲学)取得。現在、筑波大学人文社会科学研究科准教授。著書として、『権力と抵抗——フーコー・ドゥルーズ・デリダ・アルチュセール』(人文書院、2008)、『新自由主義と権力——フーコーから現在性の哲学へ』(人文書院、2009)、『脱原発の哲学』(田口卓臣との共著、人文書院、2016)など。

Images

Seiichi Hishikawa | 02
(see the section of Deputy Curators)

Venue Design

teco | Chie Konno | 29
Chie Konno was born in 1981 in Kanagawa Prefecture. After graduating from the Department of Architecture at Tokyo Institute of Technology in 2005, she attended at the Swiss Federal Institute of Technology as a scholarship student from 2005 to 2006. In 2011, she earned a doctorate in engineering from Tokyo Institute of Technology and started working at Kobe Design University as a graduate assistant. She also established KONNO in the same year. She became an assistant professor at Nippon Institute of Technology in 2013, and established teco in 2015.

teco | Rie Allison | 30
Rie Allison was born in 1982 in Miyazaki Prefecture. After graduating from the Department of Architecture at Tokyo Institute of Technology in 2005, she completed a doctoral program without degree at the same university in 2011. She has worked at Root A from 2011 to 2014 and at Atelier and I Kazunari Sakamoto Architectural Laboratory from 2014 to 2015. She established teco in 2015.

Discussion

Yoshiyuki Sato | 31
Born in 1971 in Kyoto. After competed a doctoral program in economics at Kyoto University (Ph.D in economics), he obtained his Ph.D in philosophy from Université Paris X. He is now an associate professor of Graduate School of Humanities and Social Sciences, University of Tsukuba. His published works include *Pouvoir et résistance: Foucault, Deleuze, Derrida, Althusser* (Paris, L'Harmattan, 2007), *Shinjiyushugi to Kenryoku* (Neoliberalism and Power, Kyoto, Jimbun-shoin, 2009), *Datsugenpatsu no Tetsugaku* (Anti-nuclear philosophy, written in collaboration with Takumi Taguchi, Kyoto, Jimbun-shoin, 2016).

[クレジット | Credits]

[写真 | Photo]

● 金野千恵 | Chie Konno
pp.017-019, pp.136-137, p.144

● 堀田貞雄 | Sadao Hotta
pp.024-026, p.030上(top),
p.031上・中(top・middle)

● 森中康彰 | Yasuaki Morinaka
p.028上・中(top・middle),
p.030下(bottom)

● 鳥村鋼一 | koichi torimura
pp.032-034, pp.036-039, p.052左上・
左中・右(top left・middle left・right),
pp.068-069, p.070左(left),
p.074上左・下(top left・bottom),
p.075下(bottom)

● 西川公朗 | Masao Nishikawa
pp.040-041, pp.043-045,
p.046上(top), p.047上(top)

● 筒井義昭 | Yoshiaki Tsutsui
p.046中・下(middle・bottom)

● 若林聖人 | Kiyoto Wakabayashi
p.047下(bottom)

● 仲建築設計スタジオ
Naka Architects' Studio
pp.048-049, p.052左下(bottom left),
p.054, p.055下(bottom)

● 吉次史成 | Fuminari Yoshitsugu
p.055上(top)

● 鈴木淳平 | Jumpei Suzuki
pp.060-061, pp.063-065

● miCo.
p.070右上・右中(top right・middle right), p.072左(left)

● 周防貴之 | Takashi Suo
p.070右下(bottom right),
p.072右(right), p.074上右(top right),
p.075上・中(top・middle)

● 山岸剛 | Takeshi YAMAGISHI
pp.076-077, p.078上(top), p.079,
p.106, p.107上・下(top・bottom),
p.108下(bottom), p.109下(bottom),
pp.114-115, p.118下(bottom),
p.119下(bottom), p.120下(bottom),
p.121左上・左下(top left・bottom left)

● 増田信吾＋大坪克亘
Shingo Masuda +
Katsuhisa Otsubo
pp.084-086, pp.088-090

● 長谷川健太 | kentahasegawa
pp.092-093, p.094下(bottom),
p.095下(bottom), p.096下(bottom),
p.097左下・右中・右下(left bottom・
middle right・bottom right),
p.098下(bottom), p.099下(bottom),
p.100下(bottom),
p.101中・下(middle・bottom)

● 永井杏奈 | Anna Nagai
pp.102-103, p.107中(middle),
p.108上(top), p.109上(top)

● 樋泉聡子 | Satoko Toizumi
p.116, p.117, p.125下(bottom)

● 新建築社写真部
Shinkenchiku-sha
p.118上(top)

● 伊藤暁 | Satoru Ito
p.119上・中(top・middle),
p.120上(top), p.121左中(middle left),
p.121右(right), p.125上(top)

● 出口泰之 | Yasuyuki Deguchi
p.122, p.123上(top)

● 須磨一清 | Issei Suma
p.123下(bottom)

● 坂東幸輔 | Kosuke Bando
p.124

● 増田好郎 | Yoshiro Masuda
pp.126-127, p.129,
p.131上・下(top・bottom), pp.133-134

● 濱田英明 | Hideaki Hamada
p.132上・下右(top・bottom right)

—

[翻訳 | Translation]

● Christopher Stephens
p.005, pp.024-034, pp.037-039,
pp.041-043, pp.045-055, pp.060-065,
pp.067-071, p.073, pp.075-077,
pp.079-083, pp.085-087, pp.089-094,
pp.096-104, pp.106-109, pp.115-117,
pp.119-121, p.123, pp.125-129,
pp.131-132, pp.134-135, p.137,
p.139, p.147, p.149, p.151

● Ruth S. McCreery
p.009, p.011, p.013, p.015, p.023,
p.059, p.113

—

15回ヴェネチア・ビエンナーレ国際建築展 日本館展示
en[縁]：アート・オブ・ネクサス
The Japan Pavilion at the 15th International
Architecture Exhibition, La Biennale di Venezia 2016
en: art of nexus

—

[会期 | Exhibition period]
2016年5月28日-11月27日 | May 28 – November 27, 2016

—

[会場 | Venue]
ヴェネチア・ビエンナーレ日本館（ジャルディーニ地区）
The Japan Pavilion at the Giardini

—

[主催 | Commissioner / Organizer]
国際交流基金 | The Japan Foundation

—

[キュレーター | Curator]
山名善之 | Yoshiyuki Yamana

—

[制作委員会 | Deputy Curators]
菱川勢一、内野正樹、篠原雅武
Seiichi Hishikawa, Masaki Uchino, Masatake Shinohara

—

[特別助成 | With special support from]
公益財団法人石橋財団 | Ishibashi Foundation

—

[協賛 | Supported by]
前田建設工業株式会社、YKK AP株式会社 窓研究所、
日新工業株式会社、株式会社栄港建設、
株式会社トーン・アップ、株式会社森國酒造、
株式会社安井建築設計事務所、日本工業大学
Maeda Corporation, Window Research Institute, YKK AP Inc.,
Nisshin Kogyo Co., Ltd., Eiko Construction Co., Ltd.,
TONE UP CORP., Morikuni Shuzou Co., Ltd.,
Yasui Architects & Engineers, Inc., Nippon Institute of Technology

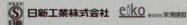

en［縁］：アート・オブ・ネクサス

—

2016年4月25日
初版第1刷発行
—

2018年3月1日
初版第2刷発行
—

編者：
山名善之＋菱川勢一＋内野正樹＋篠原雅武
—

発行者：
加藤 徹
—

発行所：
TOTO出版（TOTO株式会社）
〒107-0062 東京都港区南青山1-24-3
TOTO乃木坂ビル2F
［営業］
TEL: 03-3402-7138
FAX: 03-3402-7187
［編集］
TEL: 03-3497-1010
URL: https://jp.toto.com/publishing
—

デザイン：
刈谷悠三＋角田奈央/neucitora
—

印刷・製本：
図書印刷株式会社

落丁本・乱丁本はお取り替えいたします。
本書の全部又は一部に対するコピー・スキャン・デジタル化等の無断複製行為は、
著作権法上での例外を除き禁じます。
本書を代行業者等の第三者に依頼してスキャンやデジタル化することは、
たとえ個人や家庭内での利用であっても著作権上認められておりません。
定価はカバーに表示してあります。
—

© 2016 Yoshiyuki Yamana, Seiichi Hishikawa, Masaki Uchino, and Masatake Shinohara
Printed in Japan
ISBN978-4-88706-358-7